MERACHON

Living With The Wayuu Indians

Copyright 2016

By
Elvin C. Myers

The photo on the front cover is an aerial view of our home in Merachon. The detached garage is next to the house and the laundry room and outhouse, which backed up to each other, can be seen just on the other side of the chicken house. This photo was taken in the earlier years when we had an adobe chicken house in the back yard and a cactus fence surrounding part of yard. That fence was eventually eaten by goats. We raised chickens for a few years for eggs and meat and we also attempted to keep a vegetable garden, which is the fenced-in area beyond the laundry/outhouse building on the center right of the photo. The fence did not keep the goats and critters out so between that, the heat and lack of rain, our attempt was futile. Our enramada was being re-built at the time the photo was taken so the bundles of thatch for the roof can be seen laying on the ground in front of our home. Our five children can also be seen standing by the piles of thatch. On the far left center of the photo is the cement block building, originally built for a co-worker. Our co-workers lived there just a short time so the building eventually became our school/church building. The dirt road, that was the main road to our place, can be seen across the top of the photo and the arroyo, which was also used as a road at times, can by seen just beneath our home. On the bottom of the photo, trails that led to our home and the windmill down road can be seen. These trails were used by the Wayuu people who lived nearby and by us when we visited them. Animals also used these trails and also made their own travel trails around the area as they searched for food.

Dedication

This book is dedicated to my five children

Who endured the hardships, the separation from

Parents and home, the Help in the missionary endeavor,

and the friendships made with the Indian

Children who lived around us.

Jeanette I. Myers Briggs

Ruth E. Myers Cloud

John Paul Myers

Lynne C. Myers Thomas

Michael T. Myers

APPRECIATION

Many fellow workers have contributed ideas, photos, suggestions and encouragement to the compilation of this book. They helped me to remember things forgotten, amended what was incorrect, pointed out things they thought would be of interest to the readers, and advised the omission of things unnecessary. I am indebted to each one for their help.

Heartfelt thanks to Lynne Thomas for the hours of work on the computer in the arrangement of pages, photographs and proof reading.

My wife, Ann, typed up many of the chapters and proofread what I wrote. She also gave me many ideas for the contents.

My children read the manuscript before it went to the printer and offered valuable helps.

May the Lord add His rich and gracious blessings to each one for their interest and time in seeing this project brought to completion.

CONTENTS

Page

Preface

This book has been written because of the request of people too numerous to count who have heard my accounts of missionary life among the Colombians and Wayuu Indians of Colombia, South America. They have asked me to put them into print because they found them so interesting. To be sure, missionary life in remote areas and among primitive people is quite different than the lifestyle of Americans.

Merachon will also serve as a historical account of the missionary activity among the Wayuu tribe of Colombia, and also a record of the activity of the South America Mission.

The subject matter is not given in an exact chronological order, but it describes the various aspects of life and work among the Wayuu and the Colombian people. It answers these questions: What did we do? How did we do it? Where was the work done? Who was involved? Why did we dedicate seventeen years of our lives to do it? What were the results? What were the problems encountered? The book tries to answer these questions, but not necessarily in that order.

We also hope the book will encourage someone else to give themselves to reaching the lost. The lost are all around us. After all, the unbelieving world, whether they know it or not, is dependent on those who have light and know the truth to take it to them.

Elvin C. (Whitey) Myers

March 8, 2016

INTRODUCTION

In 1970 I was at the public library in Altoona, Pennsylvania doing some research for my class in anthropology at the Penn State University Center. Sitting at a table, absorbed in reading through the books I had pulled off the shelves, I heard a voice addressing me, "Hey, Whitey Myers!" Looking up, I saw an acquaintance I had not seen since graduation from high school in 1952. She sat down across the table from me and we had a lengthy conversation catching up on each other's past. When she asked about my line of work, I told her my wife and I were missionaries in Colombia, South America working under the South America Mission, and were in the States for a brief furlough.

Her response surprised me. "I think that's wrong," she harshly stated. "I don't think it is right to go into a foreign country and try to change other people's religion. Let them alone, they are happy the way they are. If that's the kind of work you want to do, stay here in your own country. There is plenty to do here."

It took me a moment to collect my thoughts, so I explained the Biblical approach to missions. Paul, the apostle to the world, and especially the Gentiles, went into Thessalonica, a city of Macedonia. God sent him there, speaking to him in a vision by a man of Macedonia who urged Paul to "Come over into Macedonia and help us", Acts 16:9-10. This has often been referred to as the "Macedonian Call", and many missionaries have heard a similar call in one form or another.

The Thessalonians were deeply religious people. Paul preached to them about the saving grace of God, and in response, many people in the city turned to the Lord. A church, a local assembly of believers, was established at that time. Later, Paul wrote a letter to that church and in I Thessalonians 1:9 he said, "For they themselves shew of us what manner of entering we had unto you, and how ye turned to God from idols to serve the living and true God." The gospel Paul preached to those people changed their belief system and saved their souls from a damnation that would never end and gave them everlasting life instead. It was not Paul's idea to go to Macedonia, but God's. No matter what people think about religious belief systems, there is only one way to be saved and have everlasting life, and that is to believe in the Lord Jesus Christ. People say the many beliefs are all correct; we are just climbing up different sides of a mountain but going to the same place at the top. In over seventy years of reading my Bible, I have never seen in its pages that mountain. There is no mountain in the Bible, but there is a way to God and it is through the person and work of the Lord Jesus

Christ. All other belief systems are wrong and need to be changed. Missionaries, seeing the deep darkness in which people are living, have dedicated their lives to taking the message of salvation to foreign countries. In doing so, false beliefs are abandoned and changed to sound biblical beliefs. This book is about the work of a Mission and the people who went to Colombia to minister to the Colombians and Indians who live there.

If it is argued that the words "mission" and "missionary" are not found in the Bible, let the point be conceded, but the concept is there. A missionary is an "evangelist", a bearer of the gospel, a herald of the truth, and the word "evangelist" IS in the Bible in Ephesians 4:11-12 which says, "He (God) gave some, apostles; and some, prophets; and some, EVANGELISTS; and some, pastors and teachers." For the work of the ministry in Colombia, Betty and I had four goals. 1) Preach the word so that people could hear how to be saved and pass from death unto life. 2) When people who have heard the gospel are saved, teach them God's Word so they can grow and be strong in the faith. 3) Train those who are saved to teach others and preach to their own people. 4) When they are able to carry on the work by themselves, leave. These four things we did.

This book was written by request. People never seem to tire of hearing how the Indians and Colombians lived, and how we lived, because life was so different. It is hard to relate seventeen years of missionary work and include everything, so things that I thought would be most informative and interesting are mentioned. Since so many Indians did not like to have their pictures taken, we do not have many pictures. Hand drawn maps are included to show where the places that are mentioned are located.

I especially hope to enlarge the vision of the church in America for missionary work around the world. It is the church's responsibility to take the gospel of salvation to lost and dying people. It is the responsibility of individual believers in the church to go, supported by the churches at home, prayerfully and financially. Betty and I counted it a blessed privilege to have had a share in this great endeavor.

One last word; for all the good accomplished, we give God all the honor, the glory and the praise. He opened closed doors, opened closed hearts, as His Spirit and His Word worked, and did what we could never have done in the flesh. To God be the glory!

South America

Colombia, South America

Caribbean Sea · Riohacha · Santa Marta · Barranquilla · La Guajira · Lake Maracaibo · Panama · Cartagena · Venezuela · Cucuta · Rubio · Bucaramanga · Medellin · BOGOTA · COLOMBIA · Leticia

CHAPTER ONE

Why We Went

How shall they call on Him in whom they have not believed? And how shall they believe in Him of whom they have not heard? And how shall they hear without a preacher? And how shall they preach, except they be sent? As it is written, how beautiful are the feet of them that preach the gospel of peace, and bring glad tidings of good things!   Romans 10:14-15

The Early Years

Before entering grade school my family and I attended a church near our home. We did not go often and when we did, I was not at all interested in the preaching in the worship service but I did enjoy Sunday School. After church I would go home and, when I thought no one was watching, I would arrange the living room making it the church auditorium. Pillows, coats, books and about anything else substituted for people. I would stand on the hassock before "them", and lead the song service, offer a prayer, and then preach a mighty sermon. Many years later, my mother reminded me of my early preaching days and had remarked to others that someday when I was grown, I would become a preacher. The thought never entered my mind.

At age six my family left the city and moved out into the country at which time I entered first grade in an eight grade, one teacher, one room country school. We went to church on rare occasions, usually on Christmas and Easter and perhaps a few times in between. When I was eight years old, I was invited by neighborhood kids to a Daily Vacation Bible School at a nearby church. I enjoyed it so much that I got up Sunday morning and went to Sunday School. I even stayed for the worship service. When I arrived home my parents asked where I had been all morning and I told them, "I went to church."   I stopped going to that church because there was a boy in the Sunday School class who was so totally out of control that I was afraid of him. On my last Sunday in the class, he brought his water gun and shot everybody, including the teacher, and soaked the Sunday School papers. I tried another nearby church and found it as dead as a doornail. Even at eight years of age, I could see how lifeless it was. At age nine, the pastor of the church we should have attended, visited our home. My father was working. He asked my mother to come to church because there was need of a pianist. My mother was an excellent pianist, and she reluctantly agreed to go. When my father came home from work, she told him about the pastor's visit and her agreement to go to church. My father was terribly upset; it was not the way he wanted to spend Sunday mornings, but we all went to church. Shortly after we began attending, the pastor resigned to go to another church. A new pastor came as a candidate for pastor and he was very interesting. On the way home from church I said to my parents, "I hope we get that man for a pastor. Today was the first time I sat and listened to a whole sermon." My parents agreed with me; they liked him too. In my teen age years, no one could keep me out of church. The young people who attended there became my best friends and had a profound influence on me. Their faith in Christ was genuine. One winter morning when it had been snowing all night and the wind was blowing, I awakened to a very quiet house. I checked the clock and that was the hour our house was a beehive of activity as everybody was up and getting ready for church. My father informed me that we were not going to church because my mother was sick. I looked out the window at the blowing snow; it looked so cold. I put on double clothing, bundled up real good and walked four miles to church. My parents could hardly believe I did such a thing.

I was very much involved in church activities during my high school years. After graduation in 1952 I had difficulty finding work. Altoona was a depressed city and work was scarce. I went to Washington, D.C. where my aunt and uncle worked for the government, hoping they could help me find work and a place to live in Washington. Instead, they had about five acres of land covered with an assortment of brush and they wanted it cleared off. It took me a month to finish the job. During that time, my high school girlfriend in Altoona and I were exchanging letters back and forth and, in one of them, she informed me that she was going to attend Fort Wayne Bible College in the fall. I not only never heard of the College, I never even heard of Fort Wayne, Indiana. She sent me a catalog of the College and as I looked through it, I thought that going to a Bible College and studying would be a great experience. Being involved in a ministry began to have strong appeal to me. I applied to the College and was accepted but was unable to make arrangements fast enough to get there for the fall semester, so I began my College years in January of 1953. The Lord so wonderfully provided. I went back to Altoona from Washington and found a job in a credit clothing store, working sixty hours a week for sixteen bucks. I used just enough for bus fare and saved the rest. By January I had enough for a down payment on my education. I worked during the school year and earned enough to pay for my first semester. I completed four years, graduating in 1957 with a BA degree with a major in theology and a minor in missions.

Though my girlfriend and I headed off in different directions during our college years, I will always be thankful for our Christian friendship, and I cannot help but believe that knowing her was part of God's plan for my life. She married one of my best friends in college and I met somebody else. The first time I saw Betty Bruner I was attracted to her; I asked her for a date. She very reluctantly accepted. I tried to make her my girlfriend, but she had no interest in me and told me so in no uncertain terms. Being friends was enough, but being my girlfriend did not work out – at that time. About a year later, for a reason I never understood and she never explained, she changed her mind, and at the end of my junior year we were married. I am very proud that I have made a long story short, for there is much more to it than I have mentioned, but I want to move on.

Betty had always wanted to be a missionary and that may be one of the things that attracted me to her. But how did I decide to go into missionary work? Every Friday night the College had a service called Mission Band and attendance was mandatory. Over the years at Fort Wayne Bible College, I listened to many missionaries, heard their challenges, saw their dedication, was impressed by the hardships they endured, and was stirred by their exciting experiences. I had not thought about being a missionary myself, until one winter night at Mission Band a film was shown which was produced by the Wycliffe Bible Translators. It was basically about how a missionary couple lived and worked in Peru. I was shocked to see the kind of house in which they lived. I vowed then and there that though I wasn't married yet, I would never take my wife and children to live in a hovel like that. The film showed the broken down outhouse-on-wheels they called a motor vehicle. It sometimes took the whole family to push it through mud holes, and it looked to me like it was held together by bailing wire. I further vowed that I would never subject my wife and children to a miserable existence like that. I saw the food they ate; I wasn't sure what it was sometimes. I was appalled. I thought to myself that in the United States, there are many dogs that eat better than that, and I would never, never ask my wife and children to sit at a broken down table and eat monkey meat and whatever else was being served. No siree! When that service ended, we stood to sing, "Have Thine Own Way, Lord". I could not sing. I realized that if the Lord clearly showed me He wanted me to go and do the things I had seen in that film, I had already said I would refuse to do them. Can a Christian say "no" to the Lord and then sing "Have Thine Own Way, Lord"? As soon as the benediction was given I made a bee line out of the auditorium and made fresh tracks in new fallen snow across the campus. I went directly to my room and hoped no one would come in, especially my roommate. I needed some moments with myself and didn't want to talk to anybody. Why was I in Bible College? Where was I going with my life? Was I going to do what the Lord wanted me to do, or was I going to do with my life what I wanted to do? I crawled into bed that night with huge unanswered questions in my mind. I awakened very early in the morning, and the first thing I did was make a decision. I thought deeply and long and prayed much about the Lord's will for my life. What would it be, mine or His? I came to the decision that the best use of my life and the best course to follow would be to do what the Lord wanted me to do. So, I prayed, "Lord, I'll do what you want me to do. All You have to do is show me, and I will do what You want. Not my will, but Thine! Amen!"

I had peace of mind about my decision. From that point forward I thought much about being a missionary. Betty and I talked over what we would do with our lives. Since she had always wanted to be a missionary as far back as she learned about missions, it seemed to me that God was working out the details. Leave it to Him. He's good at that sort of thing.

One day during my junior year at Fort Wayne Bible College, I went to the next step and visited the College's missions office and looked through the files. I was surprised at the number of missions listed. I pulled out some of their literature and began reading about their work which was quite varied and reached around the world. I was especially interested in South America and Brazil in particular. Among the publications I read was one called The Amazon Valley Indian published by The South America Indian Mission (now known as The South America Mission). I read an article written by one of their missionaries, C. Ray Frazier. He and his wife, Alma, were missionaries in Bolivia. The Mission required their missionaries to take a one year furlough every four or five years, and the Fraziers were asked to take half of their furlough in Colombia so that the one remaining couple there could get a much needed break. The Fraziers spent six months in the town of Riohacha, Colombia, where the Mission had a work. One day there was a knock at the mission house door and when Ray opened it, there was an Indian, dressed in conventional Colombian clothing rather than Indian attire. Ray invited him in and they sat and talked small talk for awhile as is the custom. It is considered bad manners to get to the point immediately. Then the Indian named Francisco, stated the reason for the visit. "I am a Christian", he said, and told Ray how he had heard the gospel years earlier and was led to the Lord by a former missionary. He asked Ray and Alma to come and live with his family and teach them about God. "I don't know enough to teach my family anything and I want them to know about God." Ray explained that he and Alma were in Colombia for a short time and the time was about up, so he could not honor the man's request. But Ray promised that he would pray that God would send someone who could live with them and teach them God's word.

I read that article and was greatly stirred. How, I wondered, could anyone ask to have the gospel taught to them and be denied? Standing there on the driveway leading past the college buildings, I prayed, "Lord, if You will open the doors to that country, I'll go and teach them about You." At that time, Colombia was considered a closed door country and would not give visas to missionaries. When Betty and I sent applications to join the South America Indian Mission, little did we know how God would answer that prayer. The Mission invited us to candidate school at their West Palm Beach headquarters in 1958, after which we were approved and accepted as missionary candidates. We began deputation work, visiting pastors and churches, and it took over two years for us to get promised support sufficient to make ends meet once we were on the field. Our home church, the Altoona Bible Church, took up an offering before we left that paid our plane fare and travel expenses. In February 1961 a visa was stamped into our passport at the Colombian consulate in Miami, Florida.

In 1961 we went to Colombia as a family of five. Betty and me with our children, Jeanette, Ruthie and John Paul. Eventually, two more children, Lynne and Michael joined our family, both born in Colombia.

The next morning we boarded a plane and were off to Colombia for our first term of service. By this time we had grown to a family of five and we took our three little children with us, ages 3, 2 and eleven months.

Why did we go to Colombia? We went because the Mission Director, G. Hunter Norwood, asked us if we would go there. I remembered the article in the Amazon Valley Indian and the promise I made. If the Lord would open the door, we would go. He opened the door. Francisco's request came to mind often during our deputation years. We learned that there is no person big or powerful enough, sitting behind a desk anywhere in the world who can keep the Lord from doing what He wants to do, when and where He wants to do it. We had to try three times to get the visa granted as our application was denied twice. The difference seemed to be that on the first two applications we put *missionary* as our occupation. On the third application we put *evangelical pastor* and were given visas. Why that made a difference, we don't know, but it evidently did. We landed in the large city of Barranquilla, port of entry into the country, in February, 1961, and were to be met by one of the Mission's veteran workers, Orland Corwin. But Orland was not at the airport. In case that happened, we had a backup plan. We were to take a taxi to the Geneva Hotel and he would meet us there. Word of our pending arrival reached Orland too late for him to get to Barranquilla to meet the plane, but he did show up the next day. Fortunately, the words for taxi and hotel are exactly the same in English and Spanish so there was no problem there. When we arrived at the hotel, the management did not know what to do with us, so we asked for someone who understood English because we did not yet know Spanish. A man volunteered to help with the smattering of English he knew and he understood that we were to wait there for a friend, so the management installed us in a pleasant room for the duration. The next day about noon Orland came strolling into the hotel and we had no problem recognizing him, though we had never seen him before. For some reason, Americans are obvious in a crowd. Orland looked for all the world like an American missionary. He helped us settle accounts at the hotel, and then get legally registered with the authorities. This was followed by arrangements to fly from Barranquilla to Riohacha, the capital of the Guajira, where we would live for the next twenty months. What we call states in America are called departments in Colombia. Riohacha was the capital of the department of the Guajira of Colombia. The Guajira is mostly a peninsula on the northernmost tip of Colombia and the continent of South America.

The flight in an old DC3 Colombian airline plane took a little over an hour and landed on a dirt runway on the outskirts of town. I was expecting that when we disembarked from the plane in Riohacha, the runway would be surrounded by jungle which would be inhabited by ferocious animals, monkeys everywhere and large snakes. Boy, was I shocked! No jungle, monkeys or snakes; no tigers or lions growling! Riohacha is surrounded by a dry, semi desert land covered with cactus and thorn bushes. I wasn't prepared for this, and I was not enchanted. We rode into town in the back of a pickup truck, and arrived at the Corwin house where we would stay for a couple weeks until we found a place of our own. With Orland's help, we finally located a house in the center of town and settled down to living, learning Spanish and the Riohacha culture.

Learning Spanish was our first and most important task. We had text books which we studied. The Corwins helped us many times, but our best help came from a high school student they arranged to come to our house five days a week and sit for an hour and talk with us. His name was David Correa. He was tall, very nice looking and very courteous. He helped us with pronunciation, grammar and learning acceptable customs. His help was invaluable and worth every peso we paid him. And he liked a little bit of income too. Our neighbors were also good helps in teaching us Spanish and seemed to delight in doing so. It helped to do our own shopping, mostly by pointing and grunting at first. We quickly learned not to point with our fingers but with our chin or mouth. We listened to our neighbor's arguments, of which there were quite a few, and their conversations with each other. We listened to the radio in Spanish and had devotions with a Spanish Bible. We developed a growing vocabulary and many people volunteered their help. Their helps were invaluable. It took us a long while to learn that the "ur" sound, as in mother, urgent, further and ear, does not exist in Spanish. The Colombians have a difficult time saying "girl" because of the "ur" sound. In English we have what are called sliding vowels, where one vowel slides into another, as in paper (literally pa e per. Spanish has no sliding vowels. The Spanish word for tea is "te", simple enough, but when I asked for "te" in a store, nobody knew what I was saying because I was sliding the vowel and saying "tei". It astounds me to this day that they couldn't figure it out. Our high school language helper, David, explained the difficulty. Sliding vowels changed the word we were trying to say into a different word which may not be understood. Once we were aware of this problem, we worked hard to correct it. I listened to myself on a tape recorder and was shocked at how poorly I was doing in omitting sliding vowels. By the way, the tape recorder was a wonderful help in language learning. It gave us the opportunity to hear the same thing over and over until our ears got tuned to hearing what was said. When it comes to learning a second language, the older a person is, the harder the task. Some people have an affinity for learning languages, and others do not. I suspect that I may have been in the "not" category.

After living in Riohacha for about two months, I went to the town market one morning to buy some food. An Indian dressed in conventional Colombian clothing (does this sound familiar?) stopped me in the street to converse. I knew so little Spanish that I did not know what he was saying, so he gave up trying to communicate and went his way. It was Francisco, the Indian who asked Ray Frazier to come and teach him and his family about God. I cannot tell you how badly I wanted to learn the language. I had the most important message in the world for Francisco and his family and prayed that the Lord would help me learn quickly so I could fulfill my task.

In October of 1962 we moved from Riohacha to Uribia. As far as I know, no missionary had ever lived and worked in Uribia, but may have on occasion visited since it was once the capital and they would have needed documents from government officials and offices. At one time, Uribia was named the capital of the Guajira peninsula, being designated as such because it was centrally located. But Uribia was nearly inaccessible, hard to get to with nothing more than a dirt trail connecting it with other towns, namely Manaure and Maicao. During the rainy season, it was next to impossible to get in or out of town. Since it was located in the middle of nowhere, it was too inconvenient, so the capital was moved to Riohacha. Uribia had a population of perhaps 1500 people, give or take a couple hundred. It was hard to estimate how many lived there. It was shaped like a wheel with a center from which streets stretched out like spokes in a wheel for two or three blocks. It had no town market, but people had small stores and shops in their homes. Its sole industry was the Provision de Agua, an agency that was responsible for drilling wells, erecting and maintaining windmills, and bulldozing out large holes in which water collected during the rainy season.

We were not well received when we first moved into the town, but we gradually made friends. When we left Colombia in 1978, it seems that everybody in the town was our friend and many of them had become dear to us. We lived in Uribia from October 1962 until June 1964 at which time we returned to the States for a required furlough.

One day in 1963, while sitting at my desk in Uribia, there was a knock at our door. A well dressed Indian was calling and I invited him to come in and visit for awhile. His name was Guillermo Estrada Epieyu. He was to become one of my dearest friends and a great help in the Indian work for the rest of the years we lived in Colombia. I will always be grateful to the Lord for his friendship and help, and am looking forward to seeing him in glory some day. It was not known how many Wayuu Indians were living in the peninsula at that time but it was estimated that there were about 150,000. In fact, we learned later that there were many more than that, perhaps 300,000 scattered across the land and into Venezuela. Interestingly enough, there are just thirty three last names among them, and Epieyu was one of them. At the time of Guillermo's visit, he lived about five kilometers outside of town but was working as the town jail warden. He came into the house wearing a 45 caliber pistol, unloaded. He had heard that I had Bibles to sell, which I did, and wanted to buy one. He left for home with his Bible and returned a week later for another visit. Since we were learning better Spanish, I was able to understand Guillermo and he shared with me some interesting history of his life. His father was killed in a gun fight, which was nothing unusual in the lawless land of the Guajira. His mother was unable to care for him and committed him to a Catholic orphanage. There, he learned Spanish, was well cared for and always had a great appreciation for the priests and nuns who cared for him. He told me they gave him shelter, enough to eat, an education, the necessities of life. He was fully conversant in two languages and he understood both Colombian and Wayuu Indian culture. When we returned to Colombia in 1965 for our second term of service, he had a place picked out among the Indians for us to live. We never returned to live in Uribia but lived about eight to ten kilometers from there. Before moving out among the Indians, we lived in the farming community of Fonseca, located in a pass between the Andes and the Sierra Nevada Mountains. After six months there, we moved to Carraipia where I served as pastor of the church there and also the church in the neighboring town of Maicao, about eighteen miles away. While living there, I made several trips out to where we planned to build a house among the Indians and we actually got a house started. In October of 1967, we moved to our new location where we lived the rest of our years in Colombia. We named the new site Merachon after a water hole nearby. On my first visit there, Guillermo Estrada took me to meet the Indians who lived there and who would give their approval to our living among them.

Guilllermo with his sister, his mother, and his sister's children.

Arrangements were made with the understanding that the land was theirs, and that we could build a house and a school. Some of the Indians were fine with this arrangement and others were cool to the idea. They saw no need for a school and thought we would only cause trouble. They knew nothing whatsoever of the saving grace of God. The gospel was completely foreign to them.

In making plans for building a house, I met a man in the church in Maicao who said he was part Indian, a house builder, and spoke the Indian language. He employed his two sons to help him and we hauled about 1000 sacks of cement to the building site. I contracted with a man, who could weld to make two forms from which over 1,900 cement blocks were made. Over a period of five months, the house went up. It was fifty two feet by twenty four. Though my builder claimed to be part Indian, I soon learned that he was afraid of the Indians around us and his ability to speak their language was limited to just a few words. It was hard to keep him on the job without me being there, which was not possible while I was serving as pastor to two Colombian churches about sixty miles away. With walls up and most of the cement floor laid, doors and windows in place and the roof on the building, we packed up our belongings and moved from Carraipia to Merachon. Betty and the kids had never seen the property before, so it was all a big surprise to them. With the help of two Indian men, we finished the work that was yet undone. The inside of the house was one big empty room, so we divided it into rooms. We built an outhouse and dug a cistern for water storage. Little by little, Merachon took shape and we began our work.

The back of our home that we built in Merachon. We eventually added a free standing bath house to the left and a free standing garage to the right side.

South America Indian Mission, Inc.

REV. JOSEPH A. DAVIS, D. D., FOUNDER
INCORPORATED 1921
MEMBER OF INTERDENOMINATIONAL FOREIGN MISSION ASSOCIATION

1404 FORSYTHE STREET
WEST PALM BEACH, FLORIDA
TELEPHONE TEMPLE 3-4241

January 16, 1960

The Passport Division
Department of State
Washington 25, D. C.

Gentlemen:

Mr. and Mrs. Elvin C. Myers are appointed missionaries of
this organization. They are assigned to Colombia, South America,
for a five-year term of service. Mr. and Mrs. Myers are to leave
the U.S.A. for Colombia on or about March 1, 1960.

We are responsible for their travel expenses to and from
Colombia and for their salary and support while there.

Very truly yours,

SOUTH AMERICA INDIAN MISSION, INC.

William T. Wiley

Home Secretary

WTW/W

This is our official application for a passport giving us permission to leave the country.
Without it, we would have been illegally in Colombia.

CHAPTER TWO

Documents

Let every soul be subject unto the higher powers. For there is no power but of God: the powers that be are ordained of God. Whosoever therefore resisteth the power, resisteth the ordinance of God: and they that resist shall receive to themselves damnation. Romans 13:1-2

Mankind cannot live without being governed. Government is a necessity for maintaining peace, order, judgment and protection from enemies. Men and women are placed into positions of responsibility to ensure that the laws of the land are carried out. Every country has its own system of laws, regulations and ordinances by which the citizens are governed. If a person in one country wishes to visit another country, there are specific laws to be observed in order for the visit to be legal.

Passports are a legal document, issued by a government to its citizens, which gives them permission to leave their own country to travel to another country, as a tourist, to visit other people, or to take up residence. The passport indentifies the bearer, their citizenship, and their right to protection while abroad, and gives them the right to reenter their native country. A passport can be obtained upon proof of birth accompanied by the required fee. A clean police record is often required plus the purpose, stated in writing, for traveling to another country. There are different kinds of passports. The passport for a tourist differs from that of a diplomat.

A visa is also required for entrance into a foreign country. The visa is granted by the country or countries in which one wishes to visit or reside. When visas are granted, they are stamped into the passport by a consulate officer, usually in a foreign embassy or consulate. An expiration date is of the utmost importance for both passports and visas.

Upon entering Colombia we were required to register with DAS (Department of Security). In Colombia this must be done within three days after entrance. DAS issues a very important document called a *cedula*. For Colombian citizens the cedula is a card about the size of a credit card. For foreigners it is a small booklet about three inches square which contains information from the passport, a photo and other pertinent information. When leaving the country, the cedula must be surrendered to the DAS authorities. The cedula must be carried at all times when outside ones residence. A jail sentence awaits those who are caught without it because they are not able to identify themselves. One man told us that it would be

24

better to run around the streets of the town without clothing than to get caught without your cedula. If people see you in the streets unclothed, they will simply say you are crazy. But if you are caught without your cedula, you are arrested on the spot.

Besides government officials and DAS agents, there is a police force that is stationed in most towns. Their business is to keep law and order, and sometimes they do. There is also a military police force that sets up road blocks, stops traffic and checks documents, searches vehicles for arms, contraband and anything else that might be suspicious. If the traffic is public transportation, such as a bus, all the men are required to disembark, are often searched and they must present their cedulas. Women are usually allowed to remain on the bus. The bus is carefully searched before the men are allowed to board and continue on their way.

Everywhere one travels in Colombia there are road blocks called *retenes.* Many of these are maintained by customs agents called the Aduana. Their main interest in the part of Colombia where we planned to live was to control the contraband traffic. Goods of all kinds are brought into the country illegally from the Islands of Curacao and Aruba. They enter the country by boat in clandestine places in the northern part of the Guajira peninsula, and filter down through the country, especially passing through Maicao. Some goods make it by being carted over mountain trails; others are caught along the roads and confiscated. Many people simply pay a "fine" and are permitted to keep their goods.

In Colombia I had to pay income taxes. We paid our social security tax in the U.S. but also paid taxes to the Colombian government on income received in Colombia. When leaving the country a document called a Paz y Salvo must be secured from the tax department. This document declares that taxes are paid in full up to the present time, and is presented at the airport to authorities when boarding a plane. Without a Paz y Salvo, passengers are not permitted to board a plane.

Colombia has been described by its citizens as a land of paper and stamps. This is because the government sells a sheet of paper called *papel sellado* (stamped paper) which is required for almost any kind of transaction. It has registered numbers on it and stamps, also sold by the government, which are almost always required and are affixed to the *papel sellado.* In February 1961 Betty and I had a passport for the whole family, all five of us, with a visa stamped into it, giving us permission to leave the United States and enter the country of Colombia, South America. The first time we went to the Colombian consulate in Miami, they couldn't find the order from Bogota to grant the visa. We were delayed a week in West Palm Beach at the Mission's headquarters while people at the consulate searched for it. Finally word came that the order was found and we returned to Miami to have the visa stamped into our passport. A very courteous and friendly consular officer tended to us and wished us well on our work in Colombia.

There is one more thing that is often required, namely, an assortment of shots which are registered in an international health certificate. We had all the required shots and the certificates.

On a Sunny February morning in 1961 we boarded an Avianca Airlines plane and enjoyed a flight of about two hours to the port of entry, the large city of Barranquilla.

CHAPTER THREE

Where We Lived

And when the day began to wear away, then came the twelve and said unto Him, send the multitudes away, that they may go into the towns and country round about, and lodge, and get victuals: for we are here in a desert place.
Luke 9:12

Riohacha

During the seventeen years with the South America Mission, we lived in five different locations and six different houses. Four of the houses were Colombian style adobe houses covered with plaster inside and out. Four of them had corrugated tin roofs. All had bars in the windows. Two of the houses were made of cement blocks. One had no electricity or indoor plumbing.

An aerial view of Riohacha, the capital of the Guajira Peninsula. Our First house was six blocks from the beach. A pier a quarter of a mile long extended out into the Caribbean. Ocean going ships came and went bringing in cargo and taking loads of cargo elsewhere.

When we arrived in Riohacha in 1961 we stayed with Margaret and Orland Corwin, veteran missionaries, who lived on the edge of town in a house that belonged to the Mission. Though it was at the very edge of town in 1961, by 1978 the growing city had surrounded it. It took us about a month to find a house to rent as houses decent enough to live in were scarce. Orland was our interpreter and negotiated the arrangement for a house for us in the middle of town on Sixth Street. It was a plastered adobe house with a very leaky roof. When we mentioned the leaks to the owner, he made it clear he had no intention of fixing it. His solution was "move your furniture out of the way when it rains and don't stand under the drips." One thing that helped was that it only leaked when it rained. Since the rains were seasonal, we had a leaky roof mostly in the late fall. Adobe walls have their pluses and minuses. They are very durable and cooler than cement block walls; that's a plus. They are home to rats, mice, ants, roaches, scorpions and an assortment of other creatures; that's a minus. If you have never heard a pack of rats running back and forth across a tin roof over your head, you have missed a hair-raising experience. As Nate Saint once said, "they sound like they're wearing horseshoes."

We had interesting neighbors beside us, across the street from us and in back of us. They were friendly and we liked them. The houses are all joined together, the wall of one being the wall of the next house. Our house had four rooms in the front part, a small patio, and two rooms at the back of the patio. The two front rooms were our sala (living room), a bedroom, and the other two rooms were a dining area and another bedroom. The rooms at the back of the patio were a kitchen and a storage room. We eventually moved the dining area to the kitchen room. The original dining area was the room where the roof leaked the worst. At first we had a little three burner kerosene stove for Betty to cook on. I'm not sure how to describe the stove, but probably "contraption" would be the best term. Sometimes we could not get the burners to work properly to prepare a meal. We used all the stove mechanics we knew but it seemed to have a mind of its own and worked only when it felt like it. We prayed over the stove, but it would not work. We laid hands on the stove, but it did not respond. But the Lord gave Betty an extra addition of patience and she managed. Then one day I heard that propane gas was coming to the area and gas stoves were available in Fonseca, a town three hours away over a corrugated dirt road. I went to Fonseca and bought a small four burner propane gas stove and two twenty five pound tanks. In less time than it takes to tell, we tossed the kerosene stove out. The new gas stove made Betty's task so much easier. Shortly after buying the stove, I heard that one hundred pound gas tanks could be bought locally so I bought two tanks. Betty was very conservative with the gas supply so it lasted a while. When one tank was empty, I exchanged it as

The Peninsula of Colombia

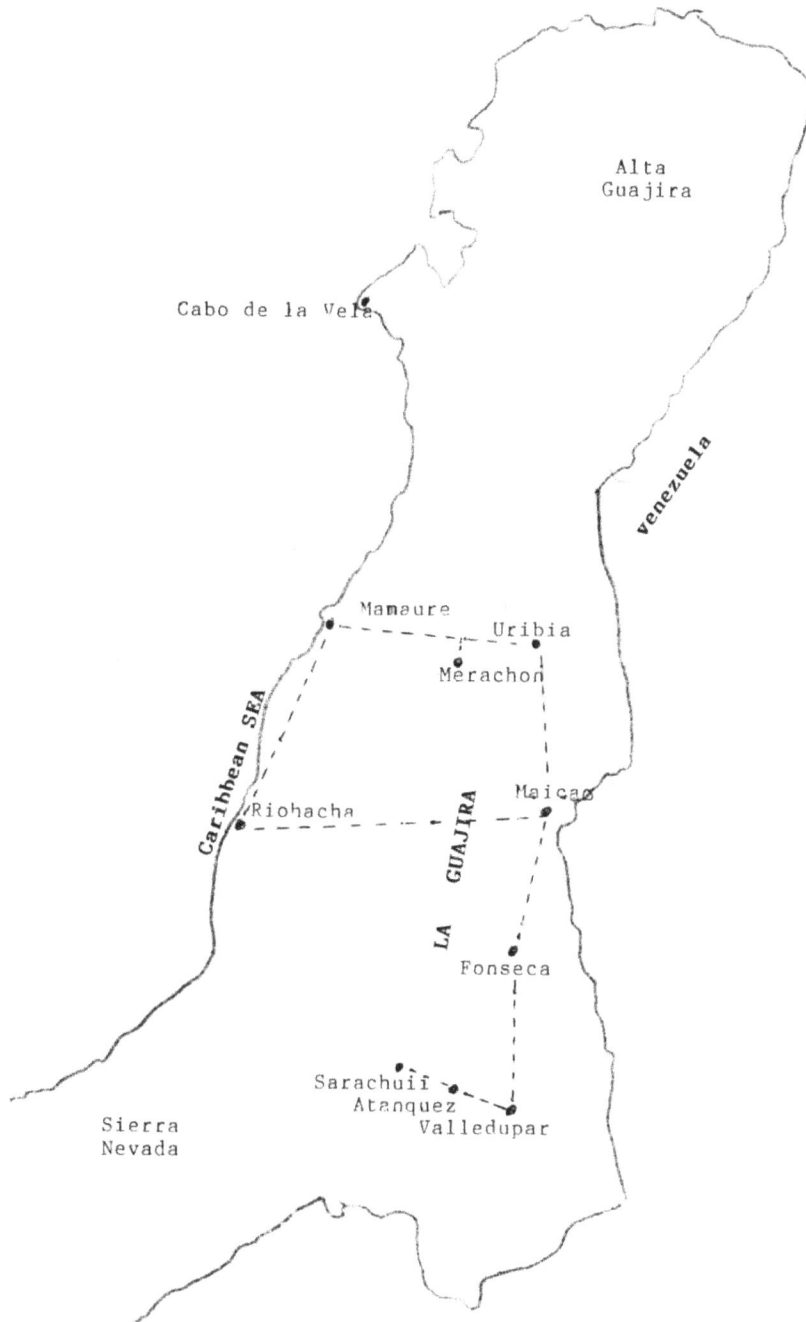

soon as possible for a new tank so we had a supply on hand all the time. We did have an indoor bathroom with running water and a sink, a shower and a toilet that went to a septic tank. The kitchen did not have running water. There was a water pipe with a faucet in the patio and we filled pans and buckets as needed and took water into the kitchen. We bought a water crock that came in two parts. The top part had a stone filter in the bottom and was filled with water that was first boiled, then cooled. The top part filtered out any debris and minerals as it dripped into the bottom part which had a faucet. It worked beautifully.

In the beginning Betty did all the laundry by hand with an old fashioned wash board. Within a year we were able to buy a washing machine which was made and imported from Venezuela. The quality was not what we were accustomed to, but it did the job, and with three small children and a dirty husband, the washing machine was a blessing that cannot be exaggerated. We continued to live without a refrigerator and shopped for fresh food daily.

Our neighbors visited us often and were curious about the things we had and saw what we could not conceal. We did not want them to see too much. They would constantly ask us, "How much did this cost?" As much as possible we tried to evade answering this question because if we told them, they would always comment about how rich we were to be able to afford such luxuries. I'm not sure why, but the comment always irritated me. In their minds eye, they saw us as so rich we didn't know what to do with all our money. Little did they know.

The street that ran by our house was dirt, but it was a main street in the town. Our house was about a half mile from the public market and six blocks from the beach. Riohacha is located on the shores of the Caribbean, and it has a pier that can receive ocean going ships. The church services were held at the Mission house, where Corwins lived, which was also about a half mile from our house. Without our own transportation we walked everywhere in town. We visited the Corwins infrequently so that we would not speak much English while trying to learn Spanish. The Corwins were always there and ready to help when we needed them.

In the culture of the area, a closed door means the occupants of the house are not receiving company. If a visitor arrives at a house and finds the door closed, they do not knock or call. You call again another time. We kept our front door open during morning hours but closed it at noon so we could eat lunch and then get naps. In the heat of desert country, naps are important; our children were small and we never had trouble getting them to sleep for awhile. When we were up from our naps, we opened the door again and kept it open until supper time. People would wander into our house like it was a public building. So, to keep our children from going out into the busy street, we put a gate in the front doorway. It worked to keep people from wandering in off the street; they would stop at the gate and call or knock and they seemed to understand, the gate was not for them but for our children.

Uribia

In October of 1963 we moved to Uribia, a small town out in the middle of nowhere. It was not our intention to move there because we had orders to move to Manaure, a small town about an hour north of Riohacha along the shores of the Caribbean. We visited the town and looked for a place to rent but nothing seemed to be available. We were asked to find a place to live there because there were believers reported to be living there. Manaure had an industry, operated by the government, of harvesting salt. Enormous pits covering many acres were bulldozed and the dirt was piled alongside the pits and flattened for a road. A canal connected the pits to the ocean and large turbines pumped in sea water. As the water filled the pits it evaporated leaving the salt deposited on the floor of the pit. When the salt reached a certain thickness and consistency, the remaining water was drained off and the Indians were called to harvest the salt. Every year thousands of tons of salt was harvested, loaded on large ships and transported to a refinery. The salt harvest lasted about a month and provided some welcome income for the Indians. Because of the torrid sun and the brightness of white salt which was hard on the eyes, the Indians worked after the sun went down and through the night and rested during the day. The pits were divided into plots and each Indian could have his own plot. They lived in makeshift structures during the harvest season which lasted about a month, and as soon as their salt was gathered they would go home.

After searching for a place to rent in Manaure and finding none, we went over to Uribia, a town inland about an hour away over a very poor, but well traveled road. In Uribia we found a place to rent and even though we were not assigned there, it proved in the end to be the best place in which to relocate. The owner of the house lived in Maicao. When we visited him to inquire about renting, he was not enthusiastic at all about renting to "evangelicals" because this could pose some problems for his business. But money is stronger than fear and American missionaries had a reputation for being honest and problem free in business matters. Arrangements were made and as soon as we were able, we moved lock, stock and barrel to Uribia. We cleaned the house thoroughly as it had been sitting empty for a while.

It was part of a building complex that at one time had been government office buildings and housing for employees when Uribia was the capital of the Guajira. The building was "U" shaped, concrete block, two stories in some parts, painted white with green trim all around, and black bars on all the windows. The property was not too shabby but was not roomy either, just four rooms. We did have an indoor bathroom which was inhabited by more cockroaches than Carter has little liver pills. What had been used for a kitchen we converted into a laundry room and we used another room for a kitchen and dining room. I put a screen door on the kitchen to keep out flies and mosquitoes.

Our home in Uribia. Two of our children are standing in the doorway in this photo.

Another blessing came after we had lived in Uribia several months; we bought a kerosene operated refrigerator. It was not large but certainly adequate, and it served us well for all the years we lived in Colombia. I paid three thousand pesos for it and when we sold it as we were leaving Colombia, I was paid three thousand pesos for it.

There was a large patio with a high stone wall around it. In the middle was a large tree called *nisparo*, which produced a small brown skinned fruit very good to eat. There was an outdoor faucet from which we got water for the kitchen. We also had an enclosure for chickens so we had some of our own eggs.

We lived in Uribia for the remainder of our first term of service which ended in July 1964, at which time we returned to the States for a required one year assignment. Our main goal while living there was to learn Spanish. It was at this time that I also made friends with many Indians. The town was surrounded by them. I would walk out into the arid, cactus covered wooded area following trails that led to their houses and make my acquaintance. Those I made friends with remained my friends all the rest of our years in Colombia.

One incident that happened while living in Uribia that will forever live in my mind was the sickness of our children. By the time we moved to Uribia our family had grown to four. I came home from an overnight trip and Betty met me at the door. The concern on her face was evident as she explained that three of our children were very sick. "Come and see right away", she said. When I entered the bedroom the three oldest were in bed and they really looked sick. They had dark circles around their eyes and were pale and could not keep food in their stomachs. We were so worried and wondered what we should do. There was a hospital in the town but it was not qualified to treat people with serious illnesses. It was more like a doctor's office. The Baptist Clinic was a long ways off in Barranquilla. We had no phone service and would not know what to tell a doctor if we could contact one. We prayed about the matter and asked the Lord to give us wisdom to make the right decision. Our decision was to wait awhile and see how they did, hoping that it was not the wrong decision. By the next morning they looked improved and the following day, were even more improved. We had no idea what caused their illness and were puzzled about it until we learned that they had eaten some beans from trees in the patio. The trees were castor trees. We investigated. According to Merck's Manual, the beans from the castor plant are poisonous; very highly toxic. Castor oil is made from castor beans, but it is carefully processed to make it usable. Five beans, according to the Manual, could be enough to be fatal. We asked the kids how many beans they had eaten and as best as they could remember, two each. They recovered nicely with no after effects, but one thing bothered us. Why did they eat the beans in the first place? We concluded that neighborhood kids had coaxed them into eating them, telling them they were good to eat. Everybody in Uribia knew that castor beans were toxic. They tried to poison our children! Years later we learned from our kids that the neighborhood kids had nothing to do with it. Our children saw the beans, wondered what they tasted like and decided to try a couple. Betty and I had come to a wrong conclusion and were glad when we found out what really happened.

We had a rough start in Uribia. No missionaries had ever lived there before and there were no evangelical Christians living in the town. We were a spectacle to the people. Nobody in Uribia was as white as we were and everybody had black hair. We were a family of blonds. When we walked down the street, people lined up at their doorways and windows to stare at us. People would come up to our children and would run their fingers through their hair. It was a friendly gesture and nothing was said though the girls did not always appreciate it. We were trying to make friends. The children turned out to be a way into people's hearts as the Colombians love children. However, people were not always friendly toward me. The town did not have a public market, but people had little stores in their homes. When I went to buy things, the merchants refused to sell to me. We went without meat for several weeks. Then God blessed us with a change which we shall mention later on in the book.

Since Uribia did not have a public market, people stocked their little stores by going to the town of Maicao for supplies. It was a hard dusty two hour plus trip over a very rough dirt road one way, that is, when the roads were in their best condition. During the rainy season, the trip would take much longer and was sometimes a nightmare. Without our own means of transportation, we relied on public transportation which was homemade buses. Uribia had three buses, which competed heavily with each other, during the years we lived there. Two traveled to Maicao daily, leaving around three or four o'clock in the morning and arriving in Maicao anytime after five thirty. Then they left Maicao to return to Uribia around ten or eleven o'clock arriving back in town around two o'clock or later in the afternoon. If it had been raining, the trip could take all day, if the buses made the trip at all. A third bus traveled back and forth between Riohacha and Uribia. It would leave Riohacha early Monday morning, stopping in Maicao on the way, and arrive in Uribia later in the afternoon. The driver would stay overnight and make the return trip on Tuesday. This would be repeated on Wednesday and Friday. When rain made the main road impassable, the drivers knew several routes through the desert that were less difficult. The drivers were experts in getting around flooded areas. Sometimes deep mud holes would require all the passengers to disembark and help push the bus. I pushed my share many times. I did not take the family on many of these trips, but made the trips to Maicao alone when we needed supplies.

Uribia did have a *matadero*, a place where animals like cattle, sheep and goats were butchered. The first time I heard the word *matadero*, I did not know what it meant. This came about when I met a young man who became my friend. I mentioned to him that we had not had any meat to eat for several weeks. He told me about the matadero at the edge of town, and knew that the next morning they planned to butcher a cow. He offered to take me over if I would be up and ready to go around five o'clock in the morning. I was up and ready. I had passed this open air building several times without knowing what it was. We walked in and the butcher, who went by the name Negro Libre, had a cow laying on the floor from which he had stripped off most of the hide and was cutting the meat into large chunks and hanging it on hooks. My friend, named Catchalero, explained to the butcher that I wanted two pounds of meat and a pound of bones (for soup). The butcher ignored me. People were coming and going and getting meat. After a half hour my friend said he had to go to work but that the butcher would take care of me, I just needed to be patient. The butcher continued to ignore me, so I asked him for two pounds of meat and a pound of bones. He ignored me. I waited several minutes and then tried again. He stood up and walked over to me, put his razor sharp knife against my throat and said, "for you there is no meat and don't ever come back here again". That was plain enough. He did not like me. About a week passed by and I was out in the street doing a little shopping. Word about my experience with the butcher spread around town. A man stopped me and told me if I wanted some meat, he would be butchering a goat at his house in the morning and he would save me a piece if I wanted. He showed me where his house was, so I went to his house early the next morning and bought a leg of goat. We guessed that the meat and the bone weighed about three pounds. From that morning forward, when that man was butchering, he stopped by our house and let me know.

I went to many of the little stores in town and was refused service in several. One lady who had a store in her house proved to be a friend over time. I walked into her store one day and, as I approached the counter, she announced very loudly so that all could hear, that she would sell me anything I needed, she was at my service. I became a regular customer at her store. During the time we lived in Uribia, people became more and more friendly and helpful. As I look back, Uribia was the right place for us to have settled. A large population of Wayuu Indians lived around the town, more than in any other area of the Guajira peninsula other than the town of Maicao. A large number of Wayuu went to Maicao every day to sell their goats, pigs, sheep and chickens and to shop. They would buy supplies to take home, one of the staples being corn. They also splurged on whisky.

Fonseca

After a home assignment, 1964-1965, we returned to Colombia for our second term of service. We lived in Riohacha for a few weeks and then moved to Fonseca. The main reason for the move was that we could not find housing in Riohacha, and the Mission had an empty house in Fonseca on Mission property. People were moving into Riohacha from the farm communities in the Guajira looking for work.

I went to Fonseca to check out the property. The house was empty and not being used. It had just three rooms but one room was large enough to be divided into two rooms. Our Mission coworkers, Harry and Norma Powell, were stationed there, living in the building that once was the Missions Bible Institute. They assured me that they would be glad to have us move up there and participate in the work. Fonseca was not surrounded with the Wayuu Indians like other towns, but they did live nearby, and we thought of the town as a temporary location. Our goal was to reach the Indians and not many were found living near Fonseca. I stayed overnight and the next morning found a truck willing to go to Riohacha and haul our belongings to

Fonseca. When I arrived in Riohacha with the news that we were moving, it was a surprise to Betty and the kids, and to the Corwins also.

Fonseca is a farming community, located in a valley between the Andes Mountains and the Sierra Nevada Mountains. The Mission had established a church there many years earlier. Harry Powell was the pastor at that time. He was a good preacher with a good command of the Spanish language which I did not yet have. It proved to be a good move for us as it helped us improve our Spanish before venturing out to live among the Wayuu tribe, a large number of whom did not speak Spanish, but many could understand it. The Powell's had four children, all about the ages of our five children and they enjoyed having playmates who spoke English. I helped Harry where I could and we enjoyed the fellowship in the work.

Our family in front of the home on the Mission property in Fonseca.

While living in Fonseca, we bought a four wheel drive short wheel base civilian Jeep to help us get around without using public transportation. The use of public transportation was always good for us because we had to use all the Spanish we knew to communicate, an excellent practice. The drawback was taking the whole family on buses, a major chore for us. Before buying that Jeep, I knew absolutely nothing about caring for a motor vehicle. I hardly knew the bumper from the hood. I had never fixed a flat tire, did not know what a distributor or carburetor were, or how an internal combustion engine worked. I began to learn. It must have been the Lord that led me to buy a Glenn's auto manual when we were on home assignment. That book had a chapter on how an internal combustion worked. I began buying mechanics tools to keep the Jeep maintained and repaired. By the time I left Colombia in 1978, I could fix just about anything except a transmission. The Jeep was a great vehicle to learn on. It was a workhorse and forgave me for much. We could not have gotten started in the Indian work without it.

Carraipia

Ray and Alma Frazier lived in Carraipia and were scheduled to return to the States for home assignment. The Mission asked us if we would move to Carraipia to take their place, so in 1967 we made still another move. Carraipia is a very small hamlet with one main road coming in off the main dirt highway that connects Maicao with Fonseca. The highway passes through three towns between Maicao and Fonseca, all farming communities. There is also one major *reten* where all traffic is checked for contraband. There are about a dozen houses around the reten, including a store and a kind of restaurant. In Carraipia, the road that comes in off the highway goes through the town and turns into a trail that goes up into the foothills of the Andes and on to Venezuela. The trail saw heavy traffic, especially those who are carrying contraband to Venezuela. In town, there were two little streets, each one a block long. There was a light plant that had a Caterpillar tractor engine that produced light for a few hours in the evenings, when there was fuel and if the engine was not broken down.

We rented a house from one of the church members. Bob and Ruth Ann Moyer had lived in Carraipia during their first term before they moved up into the Sierra Nevada Mountains. They rented this same house and had made improvements that made it a nicer house for us. There was a nice little chapel in the town and I became the pastor of a very nice flock of believers. I also traveled to Maicao, about eighteen miles away, twice a week, where I served as pastor of a larger assembly. The road seemed like it was molded on a corrugated box and it shook the life out of my Jeep, and us.

For as small as the town was, it was not a quiet town. Located about a half mile away were army barracks and the soldiers often went into town. There was no police enforcement. The law was a gun carried in just about every man's belt, and sometimes gun fights erupted. The churches of our Mission held a three day Bible conference every year. One year they met in Carraipia. A group of teens from the States were visiting our Mission work in Colombia that year and came to the conference. I gathered them together and warned them that if they heard gunshots, seek cover wherever they could find it. They thought I was telling a wild tale and trying to scare them and laughed about my warning. That same evening so many people came to the service that only about half could fit in the chapel, so it was decided to move the service outside and hold it in the street. A platform was quickly set up and the service was in progress when suddenly gunfire erupted in the next street. The people ran for cover and seconds later a pickup truck roared around the corner and down our street passing through the huddled crowd, and roared out of town. Over in the next street, a man and his son were sitting on chairs in front of their house when men in a pickup truck came

37

into town and opened fire as they drove past the house, killing both men. The incident made believers out of the teens.

We mentioned the trail that led up into the foothills of the Andes. One of our church members had a farm just off the trail. He would go up there regularly to tend to it. He was a hard working man, a sound Christian of many years, and a pillar in the Carraipia church. One day he went out to his farm but did not return home. His wife was very worried and sent someone to look for him. They found him lying where he had been working on his farm, apparently dead from a heart attack. I take my hat off to my good friend and brother in the faith, Señor Carlos Daza, a blessing to me and my family, an advisor and a man of God.

While living in this small hamlet, I was also trying to get a place ready for us to move to out among the Wayuu Indians. That was our goal. Our good friend from Uribia, Guillermo Estrada, paved the way for us to live among them. On my initial visit, a trip of about sixty miles one way, Guillermo took me to meet the Wayuu where he thought we might like to live. We all talked together about a tract of land that would be suitable for a house. The Wayuu leaders picked it for us. I continued to pastor the two churches in Carraipia and Maicao and make arrangements for this important move. It took several months before the house was ready enough for occupancy. The place was dubbed Merachon, named after a nearby water hole. I do not know if the water hole was hand dug or if it was a naturally occurring hole in the ground. It was only about twenty feet across and three feet deep when full of water.

Merachon

As best as I could understand, "Mera" means 'the center, the mark', like a bull's eye. "Chon" added onto the end of a word seems to be a diminutive form of the word. It filled with water during the rainy season. The Wayuu built a fence around it to keep out the animals. I'm not sure the fence helped. The Wayuu got their water from Merachon for drinking, cooking, washing clothing and taking baths. We drank many cups of coffee made with water from this waterhole and have lived to tell about it.

The first order of business, after making arrangements for the land, was to design a house. The plans we drew up were for a structure fifty five feet long and thirty feet wide. Before we began building we modified the dimensions to accommodate the building materials. It would be our most spacious house in Colombia.

We made our own cement blocks. I went to the factory in Barranquilla and bought 2000 bags of cement. That would be enough for the foundation, the cement blocks, the mortar, and the floor. While waiting for the cement

This is the original Merachon. We borrowed this name for our home which was about one half mile from this water hole.

Construction work on our home in Merachon. We made our own blocks of cement.

Laying the cement flooring for our front porch.

to arrive, I made arrangements with a man to do the building for me because I was tied up with the two churches. He was part Indian so I thought he would work out well in Merachon. I paid him on a weekly basis but that arrangement did not work out well. I would take him out to the building site and leave him there to work. He would take enough food for himself and his two sons who were going to help him. The next day I would find him back in Maicao where he lived, and he explained that he did not have water to work with. He expected me to stay there and bring water all day long. He was unable to solve the water problem and expected me to do it. We made a depression and cemented it to hold water. When it was sufficiently dry, I filled it with water by going to a nearby windmill several times and brought water in a fifty five gallon drum. The water ran out in two days and he returned to Maicao. He could have employed the Wayuu to bring water in clay jars with their donkeys, but I soon learned that he was afraid of the Indians in Merachon.

A view of the front of our home. The enramada in front of it, which all Indian houses have, was used for visiting and where the kids played a lot.

As time passed and the rain season was approaching, he had a trench dug and the foundation laid, along with hundreds of cement blocks, so he and his sons began laying them up. After many days the walls were up and the roof was ready to go on. I had a trucker haul in the corrugated sheets of *Eternit* for the roof and the lumber for the rafters. I had a carpenter make four doors and fourteen windows.

One thing I can say, I was pleased with everybody's work. Once the roof was on, doors and windows installed, and most of the floor laid, we were ready to move in. When the floor was finished, the builder left and we never saw him again. He died shortly after that. His wife said he died because he ate beans and onions at the same meal, and that's a no-no.

The city of Maicao is where we did our shopping and received our mail. It was a two and a half to three hours drive from our home, when the roads were good.

CHAPTER FOUR

People, Customs and Culture

Give none offence, neither to the Jews, nor to the Gentiles, nor to the church of God.   *I Corinthians 10:32*

Not everyone lives like Americans. Not everyone looks like Americans. The United States is a nation of people that have come from about every nation on the planet. In many cities, people live in ethnic groups where they speak the same language and share the same customs. The part of the city in which they settle often takes on the name of the group, like 'Little Italy' or 'German Hill'. The country of Colombia is not greatly different but perhaps not as diverse. Colombians trace their ancestry back to Europe, especially Spain and Italy, and also to Africa. Europeans came to Colombia as explorers and conquerors. Those from Africa came as a result of slave traffic. When the Europeans arrived in the country, they found that it was already populated with an assortment of Indian tribes such as the Incas, Chibchas, Arawaks and Caribs. The tribes occupied the mountains, valleys and plains; they were everywhere. The Europeans set themselves to conquering these tribes and mixing in with them which produced an interesting mixture of people. Those from Africa were added to the mixture making the people even more interesting. Today, the interior of the country shows more of the traits of the Europeans and tends to be of lighter complexion, and the coastal and northern parts of Colombia show more of the African influence and tend to be of darker complexion. This is not at all a hard and fast rule but a generalization. The Guajira peninsula consisted of all races, colors and kinds. There was a fair sized Arab population and at least five tribes of Indians.

The Guajiro Indians refer to themselves as the Wayuu, so, in the remainder of the book, that's what I will call them. As it was explained to me, Wayuu means the people. They are basically desert dwellers. The Arawaks, Kogi and Malayas live in the Sierra Nevada Mountains and the Motilones live in the Andes along the Colombian/Venezuelan border. Sometimes the Quechuas from Ecuador come up into the Guajira for business purposes. Originally the indigenous tribes of the Chibchas, Caribs, Tupi-Guarani and Quechua were the major tribes but over time they became subdivided into approximately one hundred and eighty Indian tribes, each developing their own language and culture. Today some of the indigenous people remain in a primitive state while others have adopted the Colombian culture.

The Wayuu tribe may number as many as three hundred thousand but that is a guess. If this figure is anywhere near accurate, it makes them one of South America's larger tribal nations. They cover a large part of the Guajira Peninsula and spill over the border into Venezuela. They are of the Carib ancestry and it is believed they came as warrior people to Colombia from the Islands out in the Caribbean. It is believed that the peninsula was originally inhabited by the Arawak people who retreated into the Sierra Nevada Mountains as the bigger and stronger Caribs advanced into the Guajira. While the Caribs are more aggressive and love warfare, the Arawaks are peace loving, quiet people who prefer to avoid confrontations.

The Colombians of various backgrounds settled in the towns like Riohacha, Maicao, Manaure and Uribia. There are many small towns scattered over the Guajira, especially in the foothills of the Andes and the Sierra Nevada mountain range and along the coastline in the southern part. The Wayuu do not live in towns and villages like the Colombians, but in small extended family units which are referred to as *rancherias*. A rancheria consists of an elderly couple, their children, the spouses of their children, grandchildren and often one or more who are related to the family. The Wayuu practice polygamy so it was common for a man to have two or more wives. Sometimes the wives lived in the same rancheria, and in more than one case, had their houses side by side. In the family that lived nearest us, one man had two wives who came to our house together to visit and drink Betty's very good and always available coffee. We never noticed any jealousy or contentions between them. One did the meal preparation and the other did the laundry. We noted that the Indian women often wanted their husbands to seek a second wife so their work load could be made lighter. One lady who lived near us nagged her husband constantly to get a second wife because she was tired of doing all the work herself. I am not sure how prevalent it was, but men sometimes married sisters. We knew of two cases like this. However, it seems that more often, second wives lived in different rancherias and the husband traveled back and forth. As the Wayuu learned the Scriptures, they couldn't help but notice that some of the Old Testament saints had plural wives so they did not see anything wrong with doing likewise.

The Wayuu are intelligent people. Though they live largely in a primitive state, it doesn't mean they are too short of IQ to change their lifestyle and make what we might call "progress". By describing them as "primitive" I mean that the culture is not duly affected by the advances of civilization. What I observed was that they were intelligent enough to make a way of life out of adverse conditions. Not everybody can manage in a desert. They seemed happy enough with their life style; it works for them. We did not go there to change the way they live, but to tell them how to be saved from a hell that never ends and have everlasting life instead. We noticed that they were what we call "smart" when we established a school and taught the Indian children. They were quick to learn; they wanted to learn and were very observant. Many of the older Wayuu objected to educating the children. First, they saw no need for it. At that time their language was not written down; they could not read and had no literature in their language. Second, it took the children away from work assigned to them, such as herding the sheep and taking the goats to the windmill for water, which were mostly a boy's job. The girls helped with washing the family's clothing, cooking, gathering firewood and hauling water from the windmill. The Indians had donkeys to carry the heavy water jars from the windmill and it seemed to be mostly the girls who went out and rounded up the donkeys. Girls were taught to weave and crochet, and boys were taught to make car tire shoes with woven straps. As you might be able to see, the children had a reason for loving school.

Firewood is not easily obtainable since the Guajira is desert and/or semi desert until one gets to the mountains. The foothills of the Andes Mountains begin in the Guajira, and the Sierra Nevada mountain range forms the southern base of the peninsula. Merachon had a lot of low growing trees and there always seemed to be just enough wood for a carefully tended fire for cooking. More than once we saw a man walk into the wooded areas carrying his machete. He would cut the wood and his wife or daughters would tie it up in large bundles and carry it strapped to their backs as they returned to the house. He carried the machete. A woman always walked behind her husband, never beside him. Carrying firewood is strictly a woman's job.

It was also a woman's job to bring water to the house, either from a water hole or from a windmill. In all the years we lived among the Wayuu, I never saw an Indian man carrying a large jar of water on his back in a net. The jars were carried in a net they made with a strap on it that would go around their forehead while the jar in the net hung down and rested on their back. Many of the jars were large and when filled with water, were quite heavy. The strong women often stacked one or two smaller jars on top of the large one to carry as much water home as possible. Sometimes the men would help the women lift the jars and nets into place on their backs, but the women were the ones who bore the burden. Water was not wasted. It was used for cooking and drinking. Clothing was washed at the windmill and carried home to be hung in trees or where ever they could find a good place to dry. One day I was talking to a man when his wife walked by with three large water jars, one in a net on her back, another perched on top of it which she balanced with her hands, and a third jar in a net hanging in front of her. I was amazed to see this as I knew the load had to weigh a ton. Her husband laughed and commented that his wife was as strong as a donkey and could carry heavy loads. No wonder the women get old fast! One woman who had a strong overbearing personality ordered her husband to go to the windmill and bring back some water. He obeyed. But, to make sure nobody would see him doing woman's work, he went to the windmill about a quarter of a mile away with a homemade wheel barrow around three o'clock in the morning. I heard the wheelbarrow squeaking and creaking as it went by our house. If you could have seen the wheelbarrow, you would know why it creaked and groaned under the weight of the water.

These women are filling their clay water jars in town.

The Wayuu culture is patriarchal and matrilineal. That means that the man is the head of the family; he's the boss. Matrilineal means that the children take the last name of the mother, rather than the father's as we do in American culture. In Colombian culture, children take the last name of the mother, and if the parents are legally married, also the last name of the father, thus having two last names. Among the Wayuu there were just thirty three last names. They were careful about marrying within the same family name. If the father's last name was Uriana and the mother's last name was Epieyu, the children's last name would be Epieyu.

I never learned to carry on a lengthy conversation in the Wayuu language called *Wayuunaiki*. To me the language was very complicated and I never caught on to the grammar. My talk was baby talk; the primary things people first learn to say, "Hello, how are you?" "Where are you going or coming from?" The adults made fun of me because I could not carry on a conversation. They would point to their little children and say, "they can talk, why can't you?" Betty had a better command of the language than I did, and enjoyed conversing with the young girls and school children.

45

People usually want to know how the Indians dressed, supposing that being primitive people and judging from pictures they had seen of Indians, they wore little clothing. Not all Indians run around barefoot up to their neck. The men wore a loin cloth called a *wayuucol* that was tucked in at a wide waistband in the back and front. They made their own shoes out of truck tires (there were very few cars) and woven straps which were attached to the truck tire soles with wires. Making shoes was a man's job. They had a little weaving loom for making the straps which sometimes had a pattern in them. The tires from my truck never went to waste. A Wayuu man would claim them as soon as they were too worn to be of service anymore. Their shoes lasted a long time, sometimes only the straps being changed. Even the Colombians would wear these shoes which they bought from the Indians. It was often easy to tell who passed by our house by looking at the shoe prints in the sand. The Wayuu knew who wore a Goodyear on the left foot and a U.S. Royal on the right foot. For dress up, the men often wore a long sleeved dress shirt, bought at stores in town. A prized possession was a western style hat like a Stetson. I owned such a hat that over the years had become dirty, smelly and sweat-stained, and I had no intention of bringing it back to the States with me. The elder statesman who lived nearest to us always admired that hat and asked me if he could have it as a remembrance of me when we were gone. When I handed it to him, he looked at it for a long moment, plopped it on his head and walked away. The next time I saw him, he was proudly wearing that old stinky hat I had planned to throw away. The Wayuu men also wore a little pouch attached to the waist band. The women crocheted the pouches. It was roomy enough to hold a softball. That was their wallet in which they carried some personal items. When the Wayuu went to town, the men were required to wear pants. That was the law. Some actually owned pants, but those who didn't complied with the law by wrapping the women's bandanas around them. That seemed to satisfy the law.

The women wore a dress called a *manta*. It was square dress that reached from the neck to the ankles and out to the wrists. Some of the mantas were attractive and Betty and our girls wore them around the house all the time. The manta was made from one piece of cloth, doubled over. A hole was cut in the top for the neck, and the sides were sewn up leaving openings for the arms. Pockets were sewn inside the manta rather than the outside; a belt for around the waist was also sewn on the inside of the manta. A manta for special occasions would actually drag on the ground. Many women wore truck tire shoes like the men, but they also wore a sandal of a piece of flat leather with straps attached, and a big pom pom for a fancy decoration on top of their toes. They sometimes wore bandanas which they bought in stores in town where they bought cloth. Some Wayuu women made very pretty mantas which they sold to store owners, so it was not uncommon to enter a store and find a whole rack of them for sale. Some Wayuu women had sewing machines which were prized possessions. Betty had an old fashioned treadle Singer which the women often used, free of course, but some did not know how to use it and ran it backwards. That was not good for the machine. In the end when we left Colombia, the Indians near us bought the Singer.

Wayuu women, gathered for some occasion, involved in an assortment of activities.

Wayuu dressed for a visit to town.

The Wayuu love jewelry. One of the items usually required as a dowry was jewelry. They asked for gold necklaces, bracelets and rings. A dowry was required as part of the marriage arrangement and the first dowry was paid to the man's side of the family to reimburse them for what they paid for his wife. After that, the dowries were paid to the mother's side of the family. Girls were very valuable in this respect because they brought income to the family when they married. We always found it lamentable to see the girls better cared for than the boys because of their value. A dowry usually included goats, sheep, perhaps a cow or horse. Sometimes money was required. The dowry was collected from all the family on the father's side for a son getting married. It went to the bride's family and was spread among the various members.

These are Wayuu Indians I became acquainted with during our first term of service when we lived in Uribia. They lived just outside of town and the man standing up shows how many of the Indian men dressed. The man was called "Machete" and I never learned his real name. These people were always friendly. There is a large water jar sitting on the ground in front of the women.

Divorce sometimes happened but was discouraged because half the dowry had to be returned and people did not like to give up what they had received. A lot of pressure was put on couples to stay together and fight it out. The dowry gave the marriage stability. One day two of the older unmarried Wayuu girls were visiting Betty and complaining about the dowry. They said they felt like they were being sold like goats. I decided to put in my two cents worth and told them the dowry was a good thing because it gave stability to the marriage and made the children legitimate.

Marriages were often arranged by the parents, sometimes when the girl was very young and had no idea what the parents had done. The decision about who to marry was not always hers. Usually, when a man saw a girl who interested him, he spoke to his family about it. In Wayuu culture, it is the mother's brother who is important, more than the boy's father. The maternal uncle is the decision maker. He may be asked to go to the girl's family and make a proposal of marriage. The girl's family discusses it, and if the girl is agreeable to it, they ask for a dowry and the price is not negotiable. It's a take it or leave it deal. If the dowry price is agreed upon, the boy's family gathers everything together and arrangements are made for the girl's family to receive it. It is delivered to her family and the girl goes home with her new husband. That's it. Sometimes the man stays with the girl's family. We noticed that there were some sloppy transactions made and infractions of some of their practices and these, more often than not, did not work out for good. The same is true in about any culture. Standards are expected to be observed and adhered to.

There are *mestizo* families. These are families that are mixed blood of Indians with Colombians. Family names like Gonzales, Barros, Palacio, Iguaran and Pimienta are powerful families and there are feuds between them that seemingly never end. The Wayuu like these connections with the Colombians because it gives them security. The Colombians like the connections with the Indians because it enlarges their power. The Wayuu love war and fighting. It's part of their history. Not all Wayuu Indians have connections with Colombian families.

Many of the Wayuu were not fond of going to a medical doctor. The Colombian government had one stationed in Uribia and another in Maicao. It was basically a provision for government workers, but the doctors treated everyone. When the Wayuu were sick enough, they might go, but usually preferred their own so-called doctors called the *piachi.* They could be either men or women and they practiced sorcery, of course, for a fee. We had an arrangement with the Indians that when they needed medical attention, we would take them to Uribia to the doctor or the hospital. The doctor would prescribe medicine for them and I would take them to the drug store in town to buy it. I made them pay their own bills. They always seem to have money for alcohol, so I made them cough up the money for their prescriptions. Then I would take the medicine home with me and administer it because they did not understand directions nor know how to read and do it themselves. I gave more injections than I can count. I once saw some Indians take medicine home with them, dump the whole bottle of pills on a slab and grind them into powder. Then they rubbed the powder on the infected area. It didn't help them. We never charged the Indians for any service. We were not there to make money, but to help them. We performed many medical services in our home which did not require medical training, only common sense. Two of the worst diseases for the Wayuu were tuberculosis and measles. Whole families were wiped out from these two afflictions. Indians are of the mongoloid race like the Japanese and Chinese and they do not have resistance to measles like other racial groups. This makes sense since the forefathers of the Wayuu came across the Pacific centuries ago from lands now occupied by Japan and China. When a measles epidemic gets started, it does not stop until many are dead. Those with the highest resistance survive. We tried to immunize the Wayuu, especially the children in our school, but they refused to be injected.

The Wayuu went to the piache when they were sick. The piache is often called a medicine man or witch doctor, but I prefer the word piache. A piache lived very near us and was never very friendly toward us. That's understandable because we took business away from her. They learned their practice from another piache and in this case, this Wayuu lady learned from her mother. She would enclose herself in her house with the afflicted person and commence to carry on a conversation with the devil. The devil, so they say, reveals the source of the illness, the cost of the cure, and what must be done to heal the person. Home remedies are applied; the illness may be sucked out of the body, or the illness may be pronounced fatal. If a piache couldn't heal a person, that's when the family came to us for help. That is also the time when we could get them to agree to go to a doctor. Sometimes they came too late and the afflicted person died.

We suspected the Wayuu practiced infanticide (the killing of babies). They emphatically denied this and resented our inquiries. But there was an occasion when I was building a garage alongside our house and had two Wayuu workers helping me. Part way through the day they informed me that they would not be able to work the next day because one of the babies in their family was going to die. They even indicated the hour of twelve noon when the baby would die. I was amazed that they could predict this. Betty had taken the baby and its mother to the hospital the day before and the doctor could find nothing wrong with the baby. Betty said the baby looked fine to her, smiled and cooed, and she declared the baby was not sick. That the Wayuu could know a baby that looked so well was going to die the next day, and even predict the hour, led us to think that the death was planned by the piache. When there is a death, the Wayuu fire a gun three times to advise everyone. As foretold, at noon the next day we heard three shots. If we were right about the practice, what a sad day it was for the mother. She could not stop crying but did not have the power to prevent the death of her baby, a little boy less than six months old.

The houses in which the Wayuu live are practical. They cut enough long poles to make a small rectangular building about twelve by sixteen feet, more or less. Acacia wood made the best poles for a house because termites will not bother them and it does not readily decay. The wood is very hard and will wreck a saw or machete blade quickly. It is almost impossible to pound a nail into it so holes are drilled. They are set about two feet in the ground and stand about six feet above ground. On the inside and outside small sticks are nailed horizontally to the poles about six inches apart. Once this is done, they build a hip roof (one with two sides), and the dried heart of the tall cactus plants is cut into strips, cut into lengths of about thirty inches and tied to the roof poles with string. It makes a great thatch roof that lasts for years and does not leak when it rains. On the peak of the roof where the two sides meet, just about anything will do to cover it such as pieces of tin wired into place.

Then the fun begins. A site where the ground underneath the layer of sand is especially hard, called hardpan, is dug up and hauled by wheelbarrow to the building site. When the pile of adobe dirt is large enough, they bring water from the windmill or water hole in jars and mix it in with the dirt, turning it over and over with a shovel, just like mixing cement. They let this mixture sit overnight so that the water penetrates every molecule of dirt. The next morning the whole family gathers bright and early and begins making large balls of mud the size of a saucer, which they place inside the sticks in the wall. They do this until the cavity is filled to the top all around. Then they take what is left of the mud and throw it against the wall, working it into every crack and crevice until the wall is completely covered. Inevitably, someone with bad aim, perhaps on purpose, hits someone else with a ball of mud. A mud throwing battle ensues until the workers are as covered with mud as the house. There is a lot of laughing and hollering and eventually the work is done. They install one homemade window and one homemade door. The house will have a dirt floor and will provide a reasonably cool residence for years to come. The walls will dry slowly over several months, and then some Wayuu will plaster the outside walls and whitewash them. Many times I wished that I had made our house out of these same materials except for the roof. Live and learn.

I have been inside very few Indian houses. Visiting the Wayuu is done outside the house underneath a structure called an *enramada*. It is a simple

Our neighbor was in the process of putting a roof over his enramada in front of his home.

construction with a roof on poles and open on all sides. In other words, it has no walls. Hammocks are hung underneath and the people spend the day there rather than in their houses. They sleep at night inside, but I have slept many nights under the enramadas. We had a fairly large one in front of our house and it was a busy place most of the day. So their houses are for sleeping at night, staying dry when it rains, and providing a place to keep their possessions.

The structures in these photos are called enramadas. It's the equivalent of an American living room. It is where all outdoor living and visiting is done.

The photo to the right is of us visiting our nearest neighbors.

When we first moved to Merachon, we learned that the Indians were afraid of the dark. Evil spirits come out at night and roam about freely seeking people to trouble. There was an *arroyo* which is a dry river bed that ran by our house. It ran with water only when it rained. The Wayuu told us that a spirit came down the arroyo at night, a man looking for someone to hurt. I asked if they had ever seen this spirit and they assured me they had not, but knew someone who did. They knew when he was coming because he whistled as he walked along. He was accompanied by a large black dog. I wondered how they knew this when they had never seen the spirit. They made sure they were in their houses by dark and slept with a kerosene lamp burning all night. The lamp was a cast off brake fluid can with a wick in it. It worked. I asked the Indians to let me know the next time they heard this spirit coming and I would go out to meet him. They assured me that nothing would happen to me because I am an American. Evidently being an American gives a person immunity. The spirit, they said, was that of a Wayuu man who died out in the woods and was never buried, so his spirit was angry about this and was free to wander about. He was angry because he could not join the spirit world where the departed Wayuu go. That's what they told me and were serious.

This was not the only evil spirit that worried them. One day when several Wayuu were visiting in our house, they suddenly jumped up and ran out the door and did not stop running until they got to their houses. We watched them go and wondered what brought that on; why did they depart so quickly? We did not find out until later in the day when an Indian boy who had been at our house told Betty why they left in a panic. It was because a little bird about the size of a house wren landed on the ledge above our front door. As soon as it chirped, they saw it and ran for their lives. This little bird, he said, was indwelt by the spirit of a little girl who died and her body was not buried. Her spirit was angry and roaming about freely and causing people to get sick or suffer other misfortunes. This must have been another spirit that was afraid of Americans because we did not get sick and nothing catastrophic happened to us.

Though the Wayuu were afraid of the dark, it did not keep them from hunting at night. The same cotton tail rabbit that roams the States is in abundance around Merachon. The men would go out at night hunting rabbits because that's when the rabbits came out. The Wayuu made their own shotguns. The guns were made from three quarter inch water pipe. Where ever they went, if they saw a water pipe lying around, it went home with them. They would find a small log in the woods that would make a suitable gun stock and carve the stock out of it with a machete. Then they would heat one end of the water pipe until it was glowing red hot, insert a bolt into it that just fit snugly, pound the pipe tightly around the bolt, dip it in water to cool it, and mount it on their home made gunstock. They would drill a little hole in the top of the barrel over the spot where the trigger would be, and make a mouse trap that sat on top of the barrel, designed to strike the hole. They pounded a nail into the hole so that it just protruded a fraction of

Gun sight (grease fitting)

Bolt, heated red hot, inserted into
pipe (barrel) and pounded shut.

½" or ¾" water pipe for the barrel.

Mouse trap spring

Nail pounded through
Drilled hole in barrel
and into wood stock

Bees wax

Heavy wire trigger

Ram rod for jamming a wad of paper
into the barrel (pipe) to hold powder
in place.

Wood stock carved from
any hard wood with a
machete.

Made from tin like a tin can.

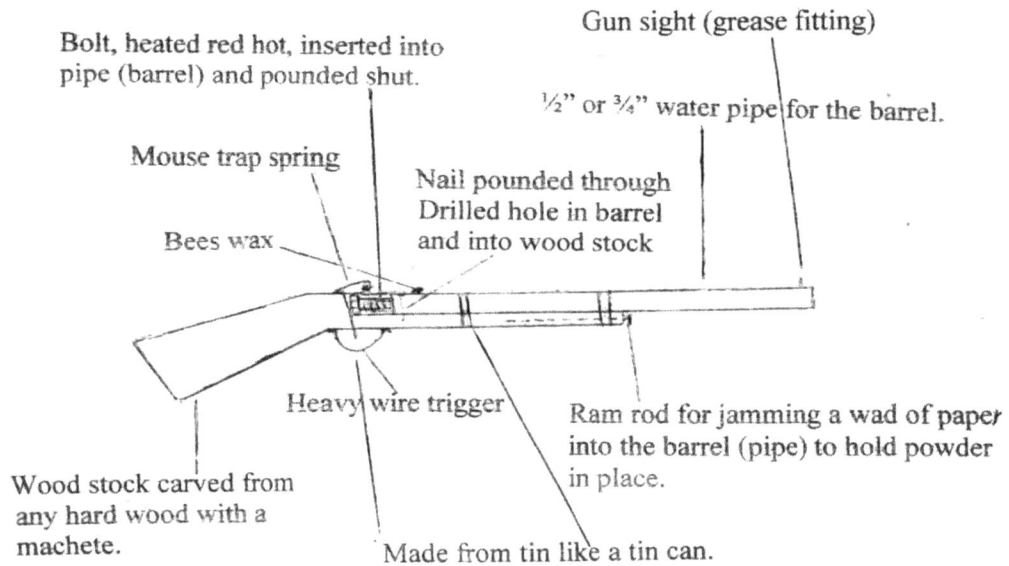

Many Wayuu men made their own shotguns from ½" or ¾" water pipe. They were very good at carving a stock out of wood onto which they would strap the water pipe with some tin they cut from tin cans. They heated a bolt until it was red hot, inserted the bolt into the pipe and pounded it closed, then dipped it into cool water. The bolt was then backed against the stock to keep it in place. A spring from a mouse trap was mounted on top of the barrel and a wire trigger attached. Some of the guns featured a gun sight on the front of the barrel made from a small grease fitting from a truck. A hole was drilled through the barrel large enough to pound a nail through and into the stock beneath the barrel. Bees wax was placed on top of the barrel into which a match was pressed with the head resting on top of the nail. Gun powder was poured down the barrel, shot, often made from discarded truck batteries, was poured on top of the powder, and a wad of paper on top of the shot to hold it in place, and a ram rod stuffed everything neatly into the barrel. The mouse trap was set, and when the wire trigger was pulled, the trap went off and hit the match head which went off and ignited the powder inside the barrel, and K-BOOM, the gun fired. Hopefully, everything held together for the next shot. It is highly recommended that making such a gun not be tried at home, or anywhere else.

an inch and placed a little patch of bees wax in front of the hole. They fixed a piece of heavy wire for a trigger that attaches to the mouse trap. When they go hunting, they place a special kind of match in wax with the match head resting on top of the nail in the hole. They pour some gun powder down the barrel, some pellets on top of the powder, a wad of paper to hold it in place, and they're set to go small game hunting. They wear a cap with a lantern on top like a coal miner wears, and when walking carefully around the woods, if there is a rabbit in the area, it is expected to be attracted to the light. When the hunter sees one, he sets the mouse trap, aims, pulls the wire trigger, the mouse trap goes off and hits the match head which in turn ignites the gunpowder in the barrel and KBLOOEY! The rabbit goes off to rabbit heaven. Do the guns work? Are the Wayuu good shots with these contraptions? We would hear two gunshots in the night and the next morning, a Wayuu would show up at our door with two rabbits. He would rather have a few pesos than eat the rabbits. The shot they use in their guns is often made from truck batteries. So the rabbit will have little shots of cast off lead battery pellets in it which must be cleaned out. Are these guns safe? Not very safe. There were occasions when the bolt would come loose and fly back out of the barrel and hit the shooter in the face. One Wayuu lost an eye that way.

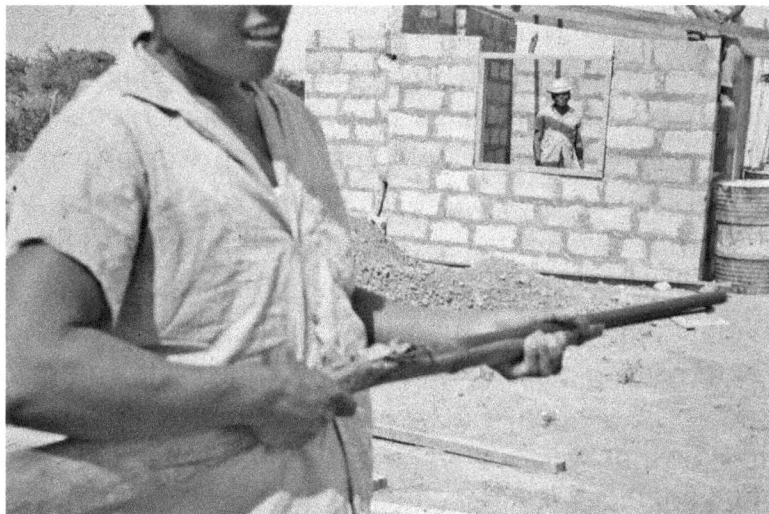

Ramon is showing and demonstrating his homemade shotgun. In the background are workers building our detached laundry room and on the back side, an outhouse for us.

The Wayuu have great eye sight and were amazingly accurate with their homemade shotguns.

Two of our nearest neighbors were Ramon and Atsira. They are pictured here with one of their daughters standing beside their house. Both became believers in later years.

It is impolite to walk up to a Wayuu house and greet the people who live there. The proper procedure is to walk up to a house and wait until they greet you. If they don't greet you, that is the same as a closed door and you leave. I would always walk up and stand quietly and wait to be greeted. Sometimes the greeting came while I was approaching the house, and other times I had to wait a minute or two while they discussed whether to greet me or not.

The Wayuu did not originally have money so they did not have their own word for it. They have money now, so they borrowed the Spanish word *dinero* but there is no "d" sound in their language so dinero became *neeru.* More about the language later. The main food staple of the Wayuu is corn. This was hard kernel field corn which was grown in the farm region of the Guajira and trucked into Maicao and Riohacha and the Wayuu buy it in sacks often weighing over a hundred pounds. The shelled dry corn is boiled until soft. Then it is run through a meat grinder, an item found in nearly every family, and ground into a gruel and mixed with water. It is stored in containers like clay jars or in pots and used daily until it is gone. Sometimes, when it's several days old, it is hard to get past the nose, but they do not waste it. The gruel, called *chicha,* is supplemented with rice, chicken, yucca, platano, beans, eggs and milk from goats and cows.

Many Wayuu families have enclosed gardens in which they plant pinto beans, watermelons, corn and a few other items. Pinto beans are one of the more important crops because they are protein. The Wayuu raise goats and sheep but rarely eat them. The animals are their main source of income. They take the goats, sheep, chickens and pigs to the public markets in the towns where they are sold, and the money is used to buy their staples. They use a lot of cooking oil, sugar and coffee. They also use the money to buy cloth for clothing, yarn for crocheting and making hammocks. Of course the men have to have a bottle of alcohol which they can't wait to drink and often arrive home dead drunk and sometimes broke, in fact, too drunk to pay their bus fare. The bus drivers usually collect later rather than argue with a drunken Indian, and they are very good at remembering who owes them. If anyone refuses to pay up, the drivers refuse to pick them up. They leave them alongside the road for someone else to give a free ride. Since it leaves the Wayuu with no way to get to town with their animals, they usually remember to pay. The Wayuu who live close to town can walk or ride a donkey, sometimes referred to as *the Guajiro taxi.* The donkeys are handy for carrying goods back home and they can carry amazingly heavy loads. They are strong and usually very cooperative. The Wayuu know exactly how to handle them. They make their own donkey and horse saddles, and they make a rack that fits over the donkey that is practical for carrying loads. The rack is especially handy for carrying water jars to the house from the windmill. These large water jars are so heavy when full that the younger girls need help in getting them loaded on the donkey and held in place while they secure them to the rack. I was at the windmill one day getting water for our house when a lady rode in on her donkey with four jars for water. Before she could unload the jars something spooked the donkey and it began to kick. It did not stop kicking until it had smashed all four water jars into a thousand pieces. The poor lady was so angry she found a good sized stick and gave the donkey a beating. Naturally, she returned home without water and had to buy new water jars.

A Wayuu woman making a clay jug which she will bake in a hole in the ground. The process takes about two days. The primary use of the jug will be for water.

Only certain Wayuu women make the clay water jars. I do not know if men are engaged in making jars. They know where the best hardpan is, which is dug out of the ground, mixed with water and made into a clay mud. The mud is carefully cleaned to remove any debris like stones and sticks. They lay a base for the jar and then carefully build it up until they have formed the sides of a round jar, except for the neck. The neck is made separately and attached to the top of the jar. The next step is to dig a hole in the ground deep enough for the jar and the wood that will be placed under it. The wood is fired up and when it is burning, the hole is covered with dirt and left to "bake" for a couple days. When the "baking" is done, the hole is uncovered and the jar carefully removed and inspected for cracks or other faults. Sometimes they are disappointed to find a hair line crack and that's all it takes for a jar to leak. If the crack is very fine and short, it can be fixed by rubbing bees wax into it. I do not know if jars with larger cracks can be repaired by applying clay and re-firing them. If they could not be repaired, they were used for other purposes like holding dry corn or rice. A wooden plug was fashioned for the neck, and sometimes a simple design was painted on the side.

The primitive lifestyle of the Wayuu was always interesting to us. On the other hand, our lifestyle was equally interesting to them. I once took out my handkerchief to blow my nose, after which I stuffed the hanky back in my pocket. Two Wayuu men who were working with me watched with amusement and asked, "Why do you put the stuff from your nose in your pocket? What do you do with it? Do you keep it for some reason?" They did not have handkerchiefs. They just leaned to one side, put their finger against their nose and blew. What came out might land on the ground, or on your nice clean floor, or on the wall inside our house. They also thought nothing of spitting on the floor and walls of our house. To teach them that this was unacceptable, Betty would immediately get some water and clean the wall and floor. They got the message.

Most of the time we found the Indians to be fairly clean. They bathed regularly and the women kept the family clothing clean. In the beginning when they saw Betty using soap to do her laundry, they asked to "borrow some". Betty would refuse their requests because she knew that if she gave just one woman laundry soap, two things would happen. First, the "borrower" would be back for more. Second, word would spread around and others would be asking for soap. There were many times when we had to say "no" to their requests as they asked for everything under the sun. Among the Colombian people there was no such thing as "a junk yard". Things were recycled down to the last bolt and nut until there was nothing left, including motor vehicles. Cars and trucks we would have junked long ago were repeatedly repaired, patched, welded, painted, wired and screwed together and kept running. There did not seem to be any such thing as "old clothing" among the Wayuu. They wore their clothing until you could see through it and then they would sew patches on it.

Everything they had was stretched to the ultimate limit. Food, like chicha, was consumed to the last drop, even if it was eighteen days old, fermented and stunk. In the States we live in a world where we discard something considered obsolete and no longer useable or in style, even before it is sold off the shelf, so it appears that we are very rich when we discard something we consider no longer useable. To the Wayuu there is still life in it.

In primitive cultures there are no clocks or calendars, yet they know the days of the week and they have words for the time of the day. They have names for where the sun is in the sky as it makes it's way from sunrise to sunset. They are very good at reading the constellations and have names for the different times of the night according to where the constellations are. The elderly do not know how old they are or care and they do not recognize birthdays. We made "birth certificates" for them when a child was born. It had the date, the parent's name, but not the baby's name, mainly because it did not yet have one. Infant mortality rate was very high. The Wayuu lady who lived nearest us had thirteen children, nine of whom died in infancy. When the parents know the baby is going to make it through infancy, they give it an Indian name and often a Spanish name. Sometimes they are given two names. Their names are sacred to them and they do not like to tell people their Indian names. The names of the elders are not used because they want it hidden from the evil spirits who will make them targets for mischief. If someone utters the name of an elder, a fine is imposed consisting of goats, sheep, chickens, money, etc. They are not stiff fines but regardless, nobody likes to pay them. Each of the thirty three last names of the Wayuu tribe has a totem sign which they sometimes tattoo somewhere on their body, the favorite place being the arm. They also believe that each family is descended from an animal, bird or reptile. So there is the rabbit clan, the rattlesnake clan, the buzzard clan, and so forth. One day when I was at the windmill getting water, several Wayuu boys were there playing a game. They would set up a large rock and then stand several feet away and throw stones at the rock. The one whose stone was the closest to the large stone was the winner. They were kidding each other about the clan they supposedly came from. "You come from the donkey clan", kidded one boy, to which the other replied, "So what, you come from the pig clan." They would laugh about this, so I jumped in to ask if they really believed their ancestors were rabbits, buzzards, snakes or pigs. Their only answer was, "Well, that's what the old people say." I pressed them for their opinion, but the first answer was the only one I got.

While the Arawak and Kogi Indians were generally quiet peace loving people, the Wayuu were an aggressive warrior type. Outside people who did not know them considered the Wayuu dangerous and hostile. Indeed, they could be. When people wanted to come to our place for a visit, we always told them not to try to find us by themselves; we would come and escort them in. The Wayuu do not comprehend that Americans do not always know and understand their culture. It is easy to unintentionally offend them which could lead to a possible troublesome confrontation. When we made friends with them, we found that they became trusted friends and seemed to understand that our mistakes were not deliberate. As the years went by, we felt more safe living among the Wayuu than we did living among the Colombians.

I think the Wayuu can drink anybody under the table. Alcohol is the cause of many of their problems. The men get together and drink, and the inevitable happens, fights break out. The Wayuu practice the rule of "blood revenge." The shedding of blood must be paid for, even if it is accidental, and even if the amount shed is small. When it happens, and the matter is too serious to settle between themselves, an arbitrator is consulted. Quite often he is a mestizo (Wayuu and Colombian) so is bilingual and knows the Wayuu rules. He helps them settle the claims by going back and forth until an agreement is reached. More often than not the price is not negotiable.

Because of the dangers alcohol brought, we made a rule of our own. When the Wayuu were drunk, they were not allowed to come to our house. Amazingly, they were very good about observing this rule. A second rule was that I would not transport alcohol in my Jeep or truck. On one occasion this rule led to a confrontation. The Wayuu would often ride into Uribia with me when I went for supplies. One day a handful of Wayuu showed up to go to Uribia with me and I noticed one little girl had an empty bottle with her. I had seen this bottle before at their houses; it was for holding an alcoholic drink called "*chirinchi*". It was a brew made in a back yard still and could be bought over the counter. I asked her about the bottle and she told me she was asked by her grandmother to buy some chirinchi for her. I told her that she could go to town with me but if she bought chirinchi, she could not bring it home in my Jeep. We went to town, I bought my items, and she bought her chirinchi. I saw her hide it among the things the Wayuu bought. I told her I knew it was there and the Jeep was not moving until she got it out of the Jeep and I didn't care how she got home. She refused to remove it from the Jeep and I refused to move the Jeep. The Wayuu went into a huddle to discuss what to do. Their decision was -- to wait me out. I found a nice comfortable place to sit and visited with people passing by. But time was passing and I was getting impatient. I went to plan "B", which was head for home and confiscate the bottle when we got there. I told the Wayuu to get on board and we went home. As soon as we got there I went to the back of the Jeep and grabbed the bottle and told the girl to send her grandmother to claim it. The Wayuu went home and in less time than it takes to tell, grandma came, a very angry look on her face and arms swinging at her sides, ready for a fight, and about ten family members with her for support. So-o, I walked out to meet her and asked where she was going. She said she was going to my house to get her bottle of chirinchi. I explained to her that the Jeep is mine and I make the rules about it, and everyone around knows I will not haul alcohol for anyone. I asked her why she refused to abide by my rules. At that point she melted and the anger left her face. She explained to me very nicely that she had no husband (deceased) and supported herself by buying and selling chirinchi. I told her I respected her business and I wanted her to respect mine also. She promised never to do it again, and thus the matter was settled which put smiles back on everybody's faces. I sent her home with her chirinchi and a hug. She respected me from that time forward.

The Wayuu are charcoal makers. They would make it where there was plenty of wood, bag it and take it to town and sell it door to door. The majority of Colombians living in the upper Guajira towns cooked with charcoal so there was no trouble selling it. It was a dirty job and the women were the sellers, walking around with sacks of charcoal on their backs. Cooking over charcoal is a science. Those who don't know how to use it waste a lot of charcoal. The Colombians had kitchens (I use the word loosely) outside their houses where a charcoal fire was kept going the better part of the day. It was too hot to have a kitchen inside the house. The Wayuu did not use much charcoal themselves; they used wood. They cooked on the ground and that is a science also. Wood is not overly plentiful where we lived so they don't waste it. A trio of rocks, some wood between them carefully manipulated, and they could fix coffee and food any time. They surprised me one time by taking ordinary field corn and putting the kernels into the red hot embers. It popped. They ate the popcorn, dirt and all.

There is a danger in cooking on the ground. One day a little girl, about five years old, who lived near us, was squatting beside the fire, unaware that her little dress was touching some hot embers. She was alone at the moment and her older sister was gathering firewood. Her mother was in town selling goat's milk. The dress suddenly caught fire just as the older sister arrived with the firewood. She dropped the wood and ran and put out the fire on her sister's dress and immediately brought her over to our house. Her burns did not appear to be severe and the girls refused to go to the doctor or hospital in Uribia. We had a marvelous salve called Ointment of Saratoga. Whatever it was, it worked beautifully on burns. We applied the ointment to the burned area on her body and she recovered quickly without the slightest scar. What a wonderful remedy. When we were in the States on home assignment we tried to get more of it but nobody seemed to carry it anymore. One drug store ordered a couple tubes especially for us.

The Wayuu do not have much in the way of furniture. They usually had a couple homemade benches and chairs around their place, but the main useful furniture, if we can call it that, is the hammock. They often have two hammocks. They keep one hammock in the house for sleeping. They roll it up and hang it from the rafters during the day and use it only at night. They have a second hammock they hang under the enramada which they use during the day. Hammocks can be bought in stores in any Guajiro town which are commercially made. But the Wayuu make their own. They make two kinds. One is a string hammock and is for common use. The other is a larger and well made hammock called a chinchoro. It is fancy and takes months to make. They are used for special Wayuu, or taken to the market and sold. They are highly prized and bring a great price. I once tried to buy one but backed away when I learned the price was equal to around six hundred dollars in American money. That was too rich for me. I slept in one once and it was like sleeping in a fine bed. I had to learn to sleep in a hammock when I arrived in Colombia. One does not lie end to end in a hammock but lies diagonally across it. It is more comfortable than it looks when used right. One thing good about a hammock, you can take up your bed and walk.

Wayuu women wove hammocks for every day use, for sleeping at night and to sit in and rest during the day.

One source of income for many Wayuu was gathering salt. In the town of Manaure, located on the shores of the Caribbean, the Colombian government operated a salt business. Huge pits covering several acres were bulldozed and a canal was opened to the ocean, allowing water to flow in and fill the pits. Powerful turbines were set in the canals to pump off thousands of gallons of water. As the salt water evaporated, the salt was left and accumulated on the floor of the pits. When the salt reached a certain consistency and depth, the surface water was pumped and the pit drained. The call went out across the Peninsula and a large number of Indians came and gathered the salt. They were paid a certain fee for what they gathered, thus supplying them with some extra income. Because of the brightness of the sun, most of the Wayuu worked late in the day, through the night and until the sun came up in the morning. It was hard work, but the Wayuu around us always looked forward to the salt season, spending anywhere from two weeks to a month in Manaure working. When they returned home after the harvest, they often brought chunks of unrefined salt with them for their daily use. We never tried using any of the salt as it did not seem clean to us. Whether it was clean or not, did not matter to them.

The main industry of Manaure is the collection of sea salt. At the top left of the picture, a pier can be seen which was used to load ocean going ships with salt.

Hundreds of tons of salt are gathered by the Wayuu Indians. They rest during the day and work in the evenings and night. Here, one lone Wayuu worked during the day.

The Wayuu work in family groups. These Indians are bagging up the salt which they will haul to the road. It will then be picked up by trucks and taken to a conveyor to be loaded on ships.

.

CHAPTER FIVE

The Desert

The sea is His, and He made it: and His hands formed the dry land.

Psalm 95:5

The Guajira peninsula of Colombia is composed of arid desert in the northern tip, semi desert in the central part and wooded mountains in the southern part. We lived in the central part which is semi desert, meaning that there is vegetation consisting of a variety of cactus plants, small trees and a wide assortment of bushes and plants. A layer of sand which can be an inch to several inches deep covers a hardpan. When the Lord made "the dry land", He made some of it very dry. It was very dry when He made it and it is still dry. The Guajira was not always a desert. The Wayuu have told us that it was once grass covered and had large trees all over. But the introduction of goats, sheep and other grazing animals, over grazed the peninsula and it turned into a desert.

How hot did it get in Merachon? We had an outdoor thermometer on our back veranda and every day at noon it registered around 102-103 F in the shade. It didn't vary much year around except in January when it would be cooler at night. Being a desert, it was a dry heat, making it tolerable, but it still sapped one's strength. The Mission had a rule that we take a siesta in the early afternoon. Sunrise began around five thirty to six o'clock, and sunset began around five thirty to six o'clock. It did not vary much during the year because we lived closer to the equator.

The trade winds were our constant companion and a necessity. It kept the temperature to something bearable, but it also blew great clouds of dust across the land. Some days were worse than others. When Betty did the laundry and hung it on the lines, dust would cling to the wet sheets and other items. She swept the floors of the house two or three times a day when the wind was especially bad. We kept our beds covered to catch the dust. At night the wind usually died down which was a blessing so we could sleep comfortably without breathing dust all night.

At meal time Betty and the girls would set the table with the dishes upside down and silverware under them. Food would be kept covered until the blessing was said. Then the food would be passed around quickly and we would eat fast enough to keep our food from getting covered with sand. On days when the wind was not so strong, we could eat in a more leisurely manner.

Our house had fourteen windows, all of which had half inch iron bars that would prevent anyone from entering through them. All Colombian and some Wayuu houses had barred windows. A house without barred windows was an open invitation to thieves. Five of our windows had a glass pane in them and these were in the kitchen area. I made screens for all the windows to keep out flies, and mosquitoes which we had during the rainy season. We did not have mosquitoes all year around in Merachon, but in the towns they were always present. Thankfully, we did not have the mosquito that carried malaria in our area. I also installed a screen around the top of the walls where it really helped, so mosquitoes could not come over the top. When we lived in the towns, we slept under mosquito nets, but not in Merachon, though we had them if needed. During the day when it rained, we did not notice the mosquitoes much, but when the sun went down, they came to life and were fierce.

This woman is getting water from an jaguey. The water will be used for cooking and drinking. They share this water hole with the animals.

The rain season was as important as the wind. The wind was necessary to cool and to turn the hundreds of windmills that covered the peninsula. The rain was essential for replenishing the underground water supply and for filling the *jagueys*. A jaguey is a depression in the ground made by bulldozers to catch rain water and they fill up during the rainy season. Some jagueys are quite large and attract wild ducks and an assortment of land animals. The Indians use the water for everything. The rain season would begin slowly sometime around September or October and continue until sometime in December. Though it often rained daily, the rain was not prolonged but often came and went in an hour's time or less. It actually could rain any month of the year, but the fall of the year was the time it rained most.

Sometimes it rained very little. That could lead to a drought. When it rained, it was amazing to watch the arid land turn green. Plants would shoot up from the dry sand producing a ground cover that provided some pasture for the grazing animals. Since the vast majority of the Wayuu had goats and sheep, the pasture was a welcome sight. The rain season also saturated the ground where the Wayuu had gardens. They knew exactly where to fence off a portion of land and plant a garden. Some places held moisture better than others. As soon as it began to rain, the Wayuu would plant their gardens. Everybody in the family had a plot. As beneficial as the rains were, they were often a nightmare for me. I had to drive on roads and trails that were often miles of mud holes. The dirt roads became as slippery as soap and it was difficult to keep the vehicle on track. Getting stuck in a mud and water hole was no laughing matter, especially if a person is traveling alone, as I often did. The Colombians who had vehicles were very good at knowing where and how to drive during the rainy season. Many Americans know how to drive in snow and ice. Colombians in the Guajira grew up learning how to navigate in mud and water. It was a science and an art. They rarely traveled alone so if they got stuck in a mud hole, they had help getting out. Everybody got out and pushed. I learned from them. The worst thing of all was having to drive at night when it was raining. Water covered the road and everything else and it was hard to tell where the road was. On two occasions I got stuck in a mud hole and could not get free. On one of those occasions I had the whole family with me. We were returning from a week long Mission conference in Fonseca and it had rained the week before we returned home and filled deep holes along the trail. I was quite familiar with the spot. When we came to the mud hole, I stopped and studied the situation. A Wayuu man showed up and showed me where to place the tires and assured me I could get through. Others had. I entered the mud hole with too much caution and nearly made it through. Notice, I said 'nearly' which is another way of saying – I didn't make it. The undercarriage of the truck was dragging in the mud. An Indian showed up with a manila rope and we tried pulling the truck ahead. It wouldn't budge. I tried as many tricks as I could think of, but all to no avail. We made a decision. The family would walk home from there, a hike of about ten miles, and I would stay overnight with the truck. They had a long three hour walk but were no worse the wear for it, walking for the most part in the dark of the night. At least it was a bit cooler. I slept in the truck over night, that is, I and the mosquitoes. I tried keeping the windows closed but it was very warm and I was uncomfortable, so I cranked the window open a little. That was all the mosquitoes needed. I closed the window and passed the hours swatting mosquitoes. The next morning, Betty informed a man who drove a bus over that road six days a week that I was stuck. He decided to see if the road was passable because he hadn't tried to drive for a week and came to where I was, declaring that the road was good between this mud hole and my house.

What some of the roads looked like during the rain season. This road was beside our home and was really an arroyo.

Travel was difficult and very hard on vehicles. This man is holding the drive shaft from the truck.

With a little effort, his bus pulled my truck out of the mud and we all headed for home. He was back in business the next morning. One thing is sure; there is no place like home! Once in the month of June we had an unusual rain. Usually our rains lasted only an hour or less. Not this one. It started to sprinkle as soon as the day dawned and increased in intensity all morning. By noon it was raining hard. It rained all afternoon and into the night, stopping around midnight. The *arroyo* (a dry riverbed that flows with water when it rains) beside our house overflowed and ran with water for the next three days. I cemented concrete blocks about ten inches high in the front door of our house to keep water from flowing in the front door and through the house. It had flowed through our house before, in the front door and out the back. This was after it had first flowed through the corrals of our neighbor's goats and sheep, so it carried a lot of "debris" with it.

We never had an earthquake where we lived but we did experience earth tremors on a few occasions. One was quite strong and shook our house so hard we thought the rafters and roof would cave in. It shook loose a ton of dust and sand that had gathered over time so everything below the rafters was covered with a heavy layer of dust, including the tables, desks, beds and all the furniture. It took all afternoon for the two of us to clean house. The kids were away at boarding school at that time.

The wind powered windmills were not always part of the Guajira landscape. While living in Merachon, the director of the government-operated Water Department in Uribia told me that up to that time, they had drilled more than five hundred wells and set up windmills to pump water. The windmills were a benefit for both the Colombian towns and for the Wayuu tribe. The Water Department, called *La Provicion de Agua,* (The Provision of Water) was located in Uribia and employed ten to twenty people. Several were Wayuu. When the crew went out to drill a well, they not only erected a windmill, but they built a large water tank that would hold several thousand gallons of water, and a long water trough for the animals, which had a pipe with a faucet that connected the tank to the trough. They also built a double sink for the Wayuu to wash their clothing. Where and how they took baths was optional. Many of them had no qualms about taking off their clothing, laundering it, hanging it in a tree and then bathing themselves. Others were more modest. Water for our house came from one of these windmills about a quarter mile away from the house. The water pipe that ran from the windmill to the water tank ran up the outside of the tank and emptied into it. I would climb up on top of the tank, which was completely open on top, put a rubber hose into the pipe and the water would run down and fill three or four fifty five gallon water barrels. I would haul it in our truck to the house and dump it into a cistern.

This is the windmill a quarter mile from our home where we got our water. All windmills have names and this one was called Arijunasain which means "civilized people live here." They must have anticipated our coming.

Arijunasain. The well was 120 feet deep. The government drilled the well, built the windmill and water tank for water storage and a trough, which was connected to the tank, for animals. The trough also served as a bathtub for the people.

Construction of our cistern, which was used for holding our water for daily use.

The cistern completed. Water was hauled from the windmill and dumped into this cistern beside our house and then a hand pump was used to draw the water up. Michael is filling buckets of water to be taken into the house to be used for cooking and cleaning. This was a daily morning chore.

To make a cistern, I had two Wayuu men dig the pit and lay a floor in it that had a depression for a sump. Then we carefully built up the walls with cement blocks and plastered them making them as leak proof as possible. I made a cement slab for the top with an opening so we could crawl into the tank to clean it. I made a lid for the opening with a lock on it to prevent visitors from helping themselves to free water. With the sump in the floor, the cistern was self cleaning, so we needed to enter the cistern only about once every three years for a good cleaning. I installed a small hand pump on the top. When we needed water for the house, we needed only to go to the cistern and pump what we needed. We had a fifteen to twenty gallon water tank inside the house and it was the boys job to keep the inside tank filled from the cistern. When all the family was at home, it took me all day making trips back and forth to fill the cistern, which was 4 x 4 x 9 feet deep. The water would last about three weeks before it needed to be replenished. When the kids were away at school, the water supply would last Betty and me two months or more. During the rainy season we did not have to go to the windmill, but caught rain water from the roof for the cistern. Nothing beats good old fashioned rain water for washing hair and clothing. It doesn't taste bad either. Interestingly enough, all windmills had a name and ours was *Arijunasain* which, we were told, meant non-Indians lived here. We were the only non-Indians called *civilisados* or civilized people, so named long before we lived there. When John Paul turned twelve years old, I taught him to drive the truck and he and Michael would drive to the windmill themselves for water. This was a great help to me. They were my water boys and never had a mishap.

70

When the Wayuu came to the house for visits or for school, they helped themselves to a glass of clean cool water from the inside water tank. Glasses were always available for them to use and a dipper hung on the side of the tank. We had to laugh as they carefully inspected the glasses and sniffed them to see if they passed the clean test. At their houses I saw glasses, dishes and cups on the ground in the dirt, which they retrieved, wiped them out with any dirty cloth like their dress, and helped themselves to something to drink or eat. They didn't have cupboards in which to keep dinnerware so their cups and glasses laid around, or hung on a nail or twig, usually unwashed. Our cups and glasses had to be clean clear through and deodorized, too.

The windmills were gathering places where news was exchanged, especially in the morning hours. The Wayuu men or boys would take their herds and flocks to the windmill for water. The goats would then be sent to forage for the day. The sheep had to have someone watch them or they would wander off and not return home by themselves like the goats. The women would take their laundry, use the water from the trough and wash their clothing on the rocks that surrounded the trough. Many of the Wayuu men and women took baths before returning home, often in the animal trough, though the more modest ones took a pail of water into the bushes for a more private bath.

Windmills and drilled wells weren't always around. What did the Wayuu do when they weren't? Children were assigned the task of following the cattle around to catch their urine. This was mixed with what little water they had and this was their drinking and cooking water. This may sound disgusting to us, but what is a person to do when water is very scarce and there is a great thirst? Necessity is the mother of invention. More disgusting than that is the brew they used to make by chewing corn and spitting it into a large bowl. When the corn was chewed and the bowl filled, it was set aside to ferment. When it was well fermented, the juice was drained off and served as their alcoholic beverage. The mash left in the bowl was fed to the chickens. We never saw the Wayuu doing this while living in the Guajira and assumed the practice ceased, especially since buying alcohol was more practical.

Sometimes the rain season did not materialize. What happened then? The land would become denuded of vegetation and the Wayuu would not be able to maintain their herds and flocks. The only thing to do was sell off many of their animals to decrease the number of the goats and sheep. A man who might have had seventy goats and fifty sheep would have had to cut the number of each herd or flock drastically.

Sheep are harder on vegetation because they tend to pull plants up by the roots when they forage, making it difficult for plants to reseed themselves.

Goats are amazing. It is not true that goats eat tin cans because they instinctively know they need iron in their blood. They eat about anything that is a plant; they are vegetarians, and their meat is especially good to eat. We had a cactus fence around most of our property which grew to about five or six feet tall. It produced a delicious fruit, about the size of a golf ball or tennis ball, with a thin skin and a blood red pulp inside. The pulp had a lot of tiny black seeds and was sweet. The Wayuu picked them with a three pronged stick because the fruit, called *yosu,* had large thorns as well as very small thorns called *pelusa.* If pelusa got into the end of the finger, it could barely be seen but it could really be felt. Worst of all, if it got into the eye it was painful and maddening. The Wayuu would pick the fruit off the cactus with a three pronged stick, and place it on the ground. They would pick off the large thorns and then roll the fruit back and forth in the sand until the pelusa was worn off; then they would cut it open and enjoy the fruit of their labor. The goats would walk up to the cactus plants, bite off the thorns which would fall to the ground, and then they would eat the juicy pulp of the plant. The thorns were long and hard as cement. Our children played with the Wayuu children and they once brought a little girl to us who had a thorn in her heel. I could just barely see it protruding and tried to pull it out. It wouldn't budge. I tried pulling it with a pair of pliers. It broke off at skin level leaving the larger part inside, and I had no way to reach it. She left the house with a thorn in her foot and I don't know what she ever did about it.

I enjoyed going to the windmill because that was like getting a newspaper. I learned the news circulating around the area. The Wayuu found the long rubber hose I used to fill the water barrels handy for filling their water jars directly from the drain pipe into the big water tank rather than the pipe draining into the trough. The water was as clean as they could get. One day a girl asked if she could fill her jars and I played a trick on her. I took the hose out of the pipe that emptied into the tank. I put my hand over the end of it. When no water came through, I told her to suck on the hose. She was working hard at it and I told her to try harder. When she did, I put the hose into the pipe and the water rushing down and hit her in the face and nearly knocked her off her feet. She was coughing and sputtering for a half hour while she filled several water jars.

When we had times of calm and the wind didn't blow, the Wayuu told me to whistle, and that would call the spirit of the wind to turn the windmill. I whistled and just then a breeze suddenly came up and the windmill began to turn. "See" they said, "It works". We all laughed because this was supposed to be a joke on me. If it was intended to be a joke, I suspect that the Wayuu might have taken it more seriously. They believe in spirits of all kinds. When it was calm and there was barely a breeze, I would spend more than an hour getting half a barrel of water. It was not possible to predict when there would be calm days and we got caught with low water supplies more than once.

Living in such conditions causes some major concerns. One is having enough water on hand and another is having enough food. Yet another concern was health. We praise the Lord for the good health we enjoyed while living in Merachon. We had very few illnesses and nothing major. When living in the towns before moving out with the Wayuu, we had a couple setbacks. One we have already mentioned was when the kids ate castor beans. While living in Uribia, I awakened one morning with a pain in my back. It did not go away during the day, but instead, got stronger. I passed a miserable night with hard pain and was getting concerned. To complicate matters there was no government doctor in town at that time. My Spanish was still in its infancy and I did not know how to explain my problem. The next morning the pain was so strong I nearly passed out and commenced to throw up. Betty and I decided it was time to do something so we asked the bus driver who went to Riohacha to take me on the bus in the morning. He refused because he said he wouldn't know what to do with me if I died on the bus. I wanted to try to get to the Baptist Clinic in Barranquilla where there was an American doctor, and thought I could catch a flight in Riohacha – if I could get to Riohacha. Others who owned vehicles refused to take me to Riohacha, three hours away. Finally, one man agreed to take me and we took off early the next morning. It was a painful trip. I packed ice around the area of the pain and that helped. When we arrived in Riohacha, the Corwins helped me by getting a ticket on the flight that morning and sending a telegram to the doctor at the Baptist Clinic that I was on my way. When I arrived in Barranquilla, Dr. George Kollmar was at the airport with a wheel chair and took me straight to the Clinic. It was a Saturday afternoon. After a brief examination, he concluded that I had kidney stones but would have to wait until Monday when the technician came in to take x-rays. The x-ray on Monday revealed that I did indeed have a kidney stone and it looked small enough to pass. It took eighteen days for the stone to travel its course. During that time Betty did not know what the outcome was or what had happened to me. When Dr. Kollmar found that out, he sent her a telegram right away. She was greatly relieved to hear something after two weeks. I cannot tell you how glad we were to see each other when I arrived back home.

The hospital experience had a hidden blessing. When I was being registered, I was told that there were no single bed rooms available at the moment, but an empty double bed room was available if I would like that, though someone could be placed there before the day was over. I asked what else was available and she told me "nothing was available except the ward room and you don't want in there." I asked what the ward room was and she told me it was a room that had ten beds, all filled but one. That's what I wanted. She tried to argue me out of it, but I insisted so that's where I was placed. I got acquainted with nine other men and I learned a lot of Spanish from them. They turned out to be as eager in teaching me Spanish as I was to learn. I am a people person.

CHAPTER SIX

Daily Routine

And whatsoever ye do in word or deed, do all in the name of the Lord Jesus, giving thanks to God and the Father by Him.   *Colossians 3:17*

While missionary husbands and wives work together, they often have different daily routines. Such was the case for Betty and me. Betty was a lifelong early riser. She was usually up no later than 4:00 a.m. Her first order of business was her personal daily devotions which she had by the light of a kerosene lamp. The rest of the family would rise and shine by the time the day began to dawn, usually around 5:30 a.m. By then Betty had done some house work, started the laundry, and was preparing breakfast. During our first term of service her work load was very heavy. Without a washing machine she washed clothing by hand with a tub and washboard. Keeping the family in clean clothing in tropical climate was no easy task, and required a lot of time and energy. Buying a washing machine half way through our first term made laundry an easier chore. We thanked the Lord often for the provision of the washer.

For several years Betty taught the children as they reached school age. When we moved to Uribia in 1962, only Jeanette and Ruthie were "in school". They had their own school desks and their school materials were by correspondence shipped from the States. Every other year we had to add a new school desk as the younger children reached school age. At one time Betty was teaching all five children. When we had our house built in Merachon, we built a school room into it. It had a library, desks and an American flag to which they said the pledge of allegiance every school day. Classes always began with prayer and reading of the Scriptures. When the children began to reach the upper grades, the task of teaching became overwhelming for Betty and we looked for another way to educate the children.

People have asked us often what the hardest thing was for us as missionaries. That's easy! It was placing our five children in a boarding school in Venezuela. It was hard for them and for us. But it was either that or return to the States for their education. They were enrolled in Christiansen Academy, better known as CA, in Rubio, Venezuela. It was a good school with an adequate staff. Our Mission helped by supplying some of the staff, mainly dorm parents. There were four dormitories; one for the older girls, seventh grade and up, and another for younger girls, sixth grade and under; and similarly, one each for the older boys and the younger boys.

One of the things that made sending the children to boarding school difficult was crossing the Colombian/Venezuelan border. It was always difficult and accompanied by much prayer. Getting the necessary documents to go back and forth was very laborious, mainly because it was so hard to get into the Venezuelan consulates to get the required permits. The Lord surely helped us make it back and forth four times each school year. Of our three oldest children, two graduated from CA. Jeanette, the oldest graduated from Altoona High during a home assignment and the two younger children finished high school after we resigned from the Mission and returned to the States.

Betty baked our own bread. Betty baked at least three times a week, and needless to say, nothing beats home baked bread. On occasion when we went to Maicao to shop, we bought bread, usually rolls called *pan de dulce or pan de sal,* in English, sweet bread or salt bread. We bought it at a bakery that had roaches, flies and who knows what else crawling around in the bread cases, so we always toasted the rolls at home.

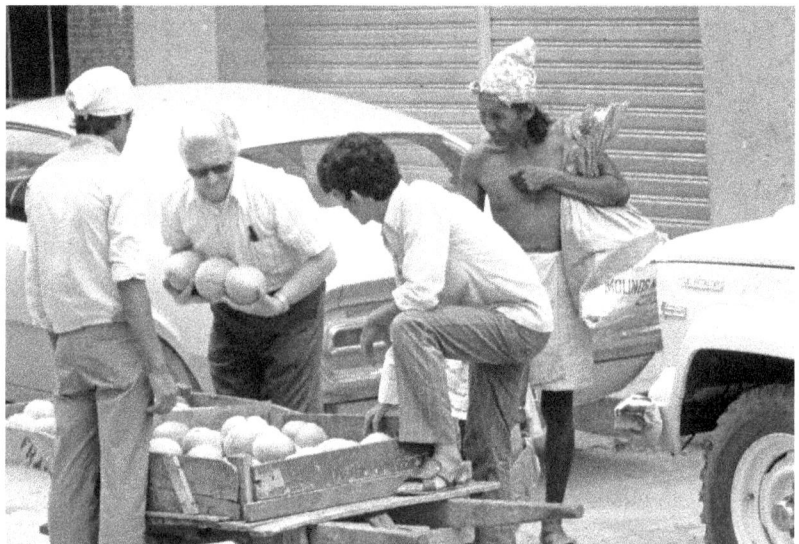

I am purchasing some melons from a home made wheelbarrel and vendor while a beggar looks on.

Before the kids went to school in Venezuela, I usually went to Maicao by myself to do the shopping. On rare occasions the whole family went along. I am ashamed to say that I had a phobia about taking my family to Maicao. I was afraid someone might try to kidnap one or more of our children. The thought terrorized me more than I can say. After the children went to Venezuela, Betty always went shopping with me which worked real well because she was a more discerning shopper than I. We made the shopping trip once a week, usually on Friday, leaving the house around 2:00 a.m. so we could get to the meat market in time to get decent cuts of meat. I would buy a block of ice and then placed the meat on the ice inside a crate which had a lock on it in the back of the truck. The trip took about two and a half hours of travel time one way when the roads were good. We always tried to visit our coworkers who lived in Maicao, Winfield and Francis Buckman, before leaving town. We would arrive back home in the middle of the afternoon, tired, dirty and sweaty. The first thing we did was get the meat out of the crate and into the refrigerator as quickly as possible. The meat had to be cut into pieces and placed in a tray under the ice cube compartment. It often began turning green by the end of the week before we could go shopping again. The green was cut off, the meat was cooked well and eaten heartily.

Another thing that worried me about taking the family on these shopping trips was break downs with the Jeep or truck. And there were break downs. We had no AAA to call for help. There was no garage to call for towing service. When I had a break down, I was on my own. I learned a lot about improvising. Once when a main spring on the front of the truck snapped, I lost the steering. I cut a tree limb with a machete and fashioned a spring out of it and tied it to the other leaves of the spring. It was good enough to get me to town. Then I drove it back home with the tree limb in place and did the repairs in my own garage. It sure made it a long, hard day. I might add here that every Saturday morning was truck maintenance time. We did not have access to lifetime wheel bearing grease, so it was necessary about once a month to pull all four wheels, remove the inside and outside bearings, wash out all the old dirty grease, repack them, clean the races, and assemble everything. I was fanatical about timely oil changes, and did complete lubrication of all parts every week. I checked tires, oil, water and brake fluids every week. I made sure I had plenty of gas. I carried water and extra cans of oil all the time. I had a tool box that stayed in the truck so I had wrenches and other tools if needed. Sometimes I did extensive maintenance on the truck, learning as I worked.

During the day Betty had plenty to keep her busy taking care of the house, the children's schooling when they were still at home, the preparation of meals, the laundry twice a week, and visiting with people who stopped by the house. We started a school for the Wayuu children and I was the teacher in the beginning. Betty eventually took over as their teacher and I was free to do other things. The Wayuu children loved her as a teacher and she had good rapport with them. The school had expanded to four grades, so she taught the younger classes in the morning and the older classes in the afternoon.

It was my responsibility to maintain the Electrolux kerosene refrigerator. The 'fridge' was only about five cubic feet and had a freezer compartment and was very efficient. Underneath was a tank that held about two gallons

Betty with a few kids from her first and second grades.

Betty enjoyed sitting around with the girls and talking, and they always enjoyed visiting with her and playing games.

of kerosene and had a wick like a Coleman lamp. The wick was delicate and had to be kept clean and trimmed. Every week I pulled the tank out and took care of the wick, filled the tank to capacity with fresh kerosene, lit the wick and placed the tank back underneath. I do not know how we would have managed to live among the Wayuu without that wonderful refrigerator. A church in Hawaii helped us pay for the 'fridge' when we bought it. The pastor of the church and a professor at the University of Hawaii, Dr. Harold Ayabe, was one of my roommates at Fort Wayne Bible College. I always tested the kerosene to make sure it had not been stored in a barrel that had previously held gasoline. Gasoline would get mixed with the kerosene and cause an explosion. This very thing happened to a lady we knew. When she went to light the wick, the tank exploded and she was badly burned. She remained severely scarred the rest of her life. Since a kerosene 'fridge' is not as efficient as an electric one, the door is never held open while deciding what to take out or put in. The decision is first made, then the door is opened, something quickly taken out or put in, and the door quickly closed. In the desert this is especially important. A special treat for a guest was a glass of cold water, perhaps with an ice cube in it.

Betty washing dishes in the kitchen. The table served as both a dishwashing and food preparation station. We had no indoor plumbing so the dishes were washed in tubs and the water was thrown out in the back yard. Note the old time kitchen stove on the far right of the photo, like Grandma had. And the roof structure like Grandma never had. Plywood walls separated the kitchen and our bedroom from the living room. The bare roof overhead was a good strong structure. A friend, Rich Mansen, is seated at the table writing and I'm reading.

If the beginning of the day began with a lot of hustle and activity, the end of the day brought a deceleration and getting ready to settle down for the night. We always ate supper around five o'clock. By six o'clock supper was over, the dishes washed and put away, and everybody quickly got their baths; I was last. The hurricane lamps were lit and as soon as everybody was ready, we sat down at the kitchen table for family devotions. We had hymn books for each one of us and we would sing some hymns in English. Then we would go around the table taking turns reading a passage of

Scripture. Then we would go around the table a second time taking turns praying. Sometimes we would have discussions on spiritual matters or something we read in the Bible that needed amplification. These were precious moments to us of family togetherness.

When devotions were over, we would play a game. Our favorite game was Rook and we had many enjoyable times challenging each other to see who would be the Rook champion of the world. Though we didn't do it often, sometimes we had a little snack to go with the game, and that made it all the more enjoyable. Snacks were special and we did not snack during the day. Since we had to go a long way for our food, snacking was uncommon, so treats in the evening were something special when we had them, usually once a week on Friday evenings. We would enjoy a bowl of popcorn, a handful of peanuts and each of us had half a bottle of Pepsi.

When darkness fell, everything was done by lamplight and candles. We had two wonderful lamps called hurricane lamps. Each one gave about as much light as a sixty watt light bulb. They use kerosene and have a very sensitive wick that can flame up quickly if a draft of air drifts over the lamp. This called for a quick adjustment of the wick until the ash was burned away which took about a minute. We used these lamps all the years we lived in Merachon. In later years I assembled a light plant that we used in the evenings, only when the kids were home from school, and usually only for a Friday night treat, or when we had company. I am not an electrician but the light plant worked very well. I was passing through the town of Valledupar one day and stopped in the co-op farm store to see what they had. I saw this generator and inquired about it. It was made in England and could produce 3000 volts of current running all day, or 5000 volts for a short period of time. I bought it and took it home. On another occasion I bought an eight horsepower Wisconsin engine. I bought some two inch angle iron, cut it into pieces with a hacksaw to make a frame and had a man with a welder weld the frame together. I bolted an old truck tire under the frame to absorb vibration, and set the Wisconsin and the generator on the frame, and a double pulley on both machines. I attached a voltage meter and wired the house. The home made light plant sat in an unattached garage. Two easy pulls on the rope and the engine started up, I adjusted the speed for the right amount of voltage, and 'let there be light'. It would run about three and a half hours on a tank of gas. When the lights began to flicker, we knew that it would be about a half a minute before it stopped. We lit a kerosene lamp to give everybody time to get into their jammies and into bed. When the kids were in school in Venezuela, Betty and I didn't use the light plant. It made noise and we liked the peace and quiet of Merachon. We used the hurricane lamps. Besides, it cost us about a dollar a day to run the light plant and that was expensive for us. When we left to return to the States, a company putting in an electric line from Uribia to Manaure wanted to buy the light plant to run an auger for drilling holes for light poles. I figured up what I paid for everything, and they didn't blink an eye at the price. They showed up the next day with the cash and I said good-bye to my light plant. The timing of the sale was absolutely perfect, so we give the Lord credit for that.

When our children were home, both before going to Venezuela and afterwards, they passed the days by doing a lot of reading. I taught the boys to play chess and they both became very good chess players. They spent some time with the Wayuu children. Many long years later, as the kids reminisced when they got together, we learned a lot of things they did that we didn't know about, nothing wrong or bad, of course, but interesting. They always went to the services in Manaure twice a week with us and took part in the services we had in Merachon, which we had twice a week also.

The Wayuu were in or around our house constantly; they came and went. The Wayuu women would stop by on their way to the windmill and chat for awhile, and Betty would serve them a cup of her delicious *tinto*. Tinto is sweet coffee. I often joined in, especially when the men came along with the women. We had a Bible study every Wednesday and Sunday evening in our house. It was mostly young people and they were the ones who were either in our school in Merachon, in a government school in Uribia or in a school at a windmill called Camino Verde. Many of them were bilingual, speaking both Spanish and Wayuuniki.

The Wayuu girls taught our girls to crochet and they became good at it, especially Ruthie. Betty kept them supplied with yarn and it kept them busy. They helped Betty at mealtime by setting the table, cleaning up after meals and keeping their rooms in order. The boys were the water boys as has been already explained. We had a good battery operated Zenith Transoceanic radio and all the family enjoyed the Christian stations that we were able to get, especially on Saturday when the children's programs were on. When I made trips to Barranquilla, I always brought home Peanuts and Charlie Brown comic books in English which they loved to read and reread until the books looked like they were chewed by a dog.

So every day was busy. Betty had the most work to do and she did it without complaint and admirably well. The kids did their chores gladly and were glad for something to do in our isolated environment. I always seemed to have more than enough to keep me busy. Whatever good we accomplished, the Lord be praised for His faithfulness in helping us and keeping us.

Betty and me with our children Michael, John Paul, Ruthie, Lynne and Jeanette on the front porch of our home in Merachon.

Betty and me in front of the truck we purchased after we returned to Colombia from our second furlough.

CHAPTER SEVEN

Dangers

For God hath not given us the spirit of fear; but of power, and of love, and of a sound mind.   *Timothy 1:7*

We were often asked if living among the primitive Wayuu was dangerous. The answer is – it could be. But it was equally dangerous living among the Colombians. Who can say it is not dangerous to live in the United States? With high levels of crime, and prisons bursting at the bars, it is sometimes not so safe in our country. Danger is anywhere and everywhere in the world. It behooves us to live wisely and trust the Lord to care for us wherever we live.

The country of Colombia has experienced times of violence in past decades, usually for political reasons. Just as the United States was at one time divided between the north and the south, and suffered through an awful civil war in the 1860's, Colombia has also suffered through internal struggles and has a time in its history known as *La Violencia,* meaning The Violence. At the time of this writing, there are still internal political struggles that affect the country. It has been the policy of Missions and missionaries to avoid involvement in the political issues of a country. We did not go to Colombia to make the country more stable, or worse, to make it more like the United States. Missionaries are committed to one main goal, and that is to teach the gospel of salvation by grace through faith apart from human works of righteousness to people who have not yet heard it. We go to evangelize the lost and win them to Christ. Once people trust the Lord for salvation, the next step is to teach them God's word to establish them in sound faith.

However, back to the question; did we encounter dangers? There were indeed some situations that could have gone badly for us. Some situations were worse than others. Though the Guajira peninsula had police stationed in some of the towns, and there were some army bases scattered around the peninsula, the state tended to be somewhat lawless. Neither the police nor the military seemed to bother with the Wayuu who had their own rules of conduct, especially the law of blood revenge. The shedding of blood always had to be paid for and it was usually by retaliation. The law was, more often than not, an assortment of pistols and revolvers which were carried in the belt of many men, and they didn't hesitate to use them. Gunfights were common, and many Colombian and Wayuu families were plagued with enemies. Long standing wars and quarrels never seemed to end. Among the warrior prone Wayuu were quarrels that had been going on for years, so we as missionaries had to be careful never to involve ourselves in their feuds or we could become victims. For the Indians, guns were their weapons of choice and they were well armed. This means that they could not travel freely anywhere they wished around the peninsula for fear of encountering enemies. They were very proud of their guns. One man showed me his rifle; on the side it said "Mexican/American War".

One day a large band of Wayuu on horses raced by our house. Shortly after that, I went to the windmill for water and these Indians were there taking baths, watering their horses, and in general, resting before moving on. There were at least thirty men and some of them were drunk. A couple of them came over to the truck to talk and then went their way. One Wayuu, who was very drunk and mounted on his horse, came over to the truck and asked me a question I did not understand, so I unwisely said "yes". What he asked me was to take a drink with him and handed me his bottle. When he saw that I did not take a drink, he was offended. He had a beautiful Winchester rifle in his saddle holster which he pulled out and made sure it was loaded. I knew I was in trouble. Some Wayuu from around our place, who had been washing clothing, quickly gathered their things together and left. The drunken Indian was talking to them and I could tell they were concerned about what he was saying. As our neighbors passed our house, they stopped to tell Betty that this man said I had offended him by refusing to drink with him and he was going to kill me. Word spread quickly and neighbors came running to our house. They were listening for gunshots. All the band of Wayuu had left the windmill except this one drunken man. Suddenly, one of the men from the band came back for him and a lengthy conversation took place. He convinced his drunken companion that I was an American and that he would get into real big trouble if he shot me. He talked the drunken Wayuu out of shooting me and left with him in tow. I got my water and went home and was met by several neighbors and one relieved wife. They themselves did not know who these Wayuu were but were afraid when they saw them in the area. They know their own people.

On another occasion a band of robbers, who were part Wayuu and part Colombian, laid wait for us as we went to Maicao to shop. They had learned our schedule. We went to Maicao every Friday morning. There is no doubt that they would have killed Betty and me and taken the truck. They were waiting beside a Wayuu house along the road and the man who lived there heard them talking about their plans. As I passed by they came running out to the road giving the impression that they wanted a ride to Maicao. What they wanted was for me to stop and they would carry out their plans. I didn't stop and they didn't make a great effort to stop me. The Wayuu who lived in that house went to Uribia and informed a lady about the danger I was in. She called me into town, took me aside where no one could hear or was looking on and told me of these men and their plans. She said that what saved me that morning was that I had Wayuu passengers in my truck and the robbers did not want to get involved with them. Does the Lord watch over us or what!

One day when I went to Maicao to do some shopping, I took with me my two sons, John Paul and Michael. The truck got a flat tire on the way so I put on the spare. When we got to town I went to the shop that did nothing but fix flat tires. John Paul waited in the cab and Michael was in the back of the truck sitting on a large crate. Suddenly there was an eruption of gunfire behind the truck. Two men were firing away at each other. Doors and windows slammed shut while the gun fight went on. John Paul crawled under the dash for safety. Michael sat on the crate watching the gunfight. I yelled at him to get down behind the crate. He said, "What for? They're not shooting at me." One man went down and the other fled. I watched the man in the gutter from my hiding place. I saw him slowly raise his head and look around. He jumped up and took off running. I didn't see blood anywhere so assumed that though both men had emptied their guns, no one was hit.

Many men died of "lead poisoning" (bullets) in the Guajira. People, including the army stationed in Uribia, wondered why I didn't own a gun. I explained that I was not in Colombia to kill people or even defend myself. I was there to preach the gospel of the Lord Jesus Christ. The army came out to our house one time to see what we were all about. They offered to 'give' me a gun, free of charge, but I would have to buy the ammunition. I thanked them, but "no thanks".

A large boa constrictor I dragged out of a ditch thinking it was dead. It wasn't. My friend, John Bremen, took the picture and we let the snake go.

There was the danger of getting lost in the area where we lived. One morning I looked out on our back porch and saw a Wayuu standing there. I went out to see who he was and what he wanted. He was lost. He was covered with scratches and had a little boy with him, about age eight, also covered with scratches. He took a trail he thought he knew and before he realized it, the sun was setting. They had been in the woods all night wandering around. Betty gave them something to eat and drink. I tried to determine where they lived and drove them part way to their house; part way because there was no trail to their house over which I could drive.

When it rained, water covered the land so that trails were indistinguishable. I had to walk to and from town several times over the years, perhaps an eight mile hike through the wooded areas. Once I made a foolish decision to take a short cut a Wayuu showed me. What started out as a clear path soon became a water covered path. I should have turned around right there and retraced my steps. Instead, I continued on, thinking I would run out of the water. But the water got deeper. It was over my ankles. When it was nearly up to my knees and I couldn't actually see any path anymore, I decided to go back the way I came. But, when I turned around, all I could see was water and couldn't tell where I had walked. So I pressed on until the water was over my knees. Then I came to a fence which meant that somebody had a garden so I knew there must be a house nearby. I walked around the fence and never saw a house. I saw a trail that led away from the garden and followed it. I was lost. I had no idea where I was or where the path led to, but at least I was gradually walking out of the water. Finally I came to a road. I was puzzled. What road was this? I looked up and down the road and nothing looked familiar. I decided to go to my right and in a matter of a few minutes I came to a tree I recognized. I knew where I was, turned around and followed the road home. To this day, I have no idea where I was, who the fenced in garden belonged to or who lived nearby. I learned a lesson the hard way; stick to well known roads and trails. It is easy to get lost in the kind of terrain where Merachon was located. I'm embarrassed to say this, but I did not learn my lesson very well. About a year later I was walking on an unknown trail to a Wayuu rancheria about two miles away and it began to rain. It poured. I heard some Wayuu heading my way and could tell they were drunk. I stepped off the path and hid until they passed by. When I stepped out to the path, it was so covered by water I couldn't find it. I never found it again and wandered around for two hours looking for something familiar. I tried a trick. I barked like a dog. It worked. A dog answered me and I knew it meant a Wayuu rancheria was nearby. I found it in the pouring rain. The Wayuu who lived there were those I knew well and they were surprised to see me. They were wondering what I was doing walking around in the rain. Judging by the direction I had come from to their house, they knew I had been lost and they had a great time kidding me about it. After some coffee and some good hearted laughter, I headed for home in the rain, and of course, the rain stopped about the time I reached Merachon.

I did not wander far from home when I was alone. There was always the danger of meeting Wayuu who did not know me, and there were those who were not exactly trustworthy. It could be especially dangerous if they had been drinking. We had a rule that when the Wayuu were drinking they were not to come to our house but there were two older men who often came drunk or sober anyway. They were harmless and we decided not to make an issue with them. An unknown Wayuu came one day holding a cloth over his eye. I took at look at it and it looked bad to me. I drove him to Uribia and just as I pulled up to the hospital, the doctor was coming out the door. We went into his office and he looked at the eye and said it could not be saved. The story was that the man had been drinking and tried to walk home in the dark. He stumbled and fell, running a tree branch into his eye. Since there was no infection or complication with the eye, the doctor put a patch over it and told the Wayuu to leave it there for a couple days and it would heal over.

Another danger in our area was snakes. There were so many of them, small, big, poisonous and some we didn't even know what they were. We had the eastern diamondback rattlesnake and a variety of coral snakes

The most common venomous snake was the fer-de-lance, an aggressive poisonous snake. Because of the desert sun and heat, most snakes tended to be nocturnal and were therefore not often seen, that is, until it was too late. During the rainy season their underground dens would fill with water and drive them out into the bushes and trees.

When I had meetings with boys and men here in the States, one question asked most, especially by the boys, was "did you ever see any big snakes?" I saw at least eight snakes that were ten feet or longer. On one occasion I encountered an anaconda that had to be a minimum of twelve feet crawling down the middle of the road I was traveling. It was huge. I didn't get out of my Jeep to measure it to be sure. It was the only anaconda I saw in the wild and I only ever saw one bushmaster, about a four footer. I personally knew three people who died from snake bites and I can testify, it's a hard way to go.

Besides the number of snakes in our area, there was one critter we all feared and that was the *kaseepa*. This was a very large centipede reaching easily eight inches or more, wide as a thumb minus the legs, and was poisonous. It had three sets of jaws and a terrible bite. I never heard of anyone dying from the bite of a centipede, but the wound they inflicted took a long time to heal and sometimes left a scar. Fortunately, I was the only one in our family that was ever bitten. I was awakened one night when one bit me on the knee. It was not a severe bite but it took two months to heal and it left a mark on my knee for a couple years. The centipede took just a little taste and would have moved on but I never gave it a chance. I chased it around until I cornered it and smashed it with a hammer as flat as a ribbon. Twice I put on my trousers and found one inside the pant leg. A baby centipede crawled on Ruthie's neck one night and I brushed it off and dispatched it quickly. On another occasion, an evening when we had returned home from an evening service with the Wayuu in Manaure, I saw a centipede on the wall above the kids beds. It was enormous, the granddaddy of them all. I estimated it to be about ten inches long. I wanted to catch it and preserve it in a bottle of formalin. Try as I did, it was too elusive and I could not catch it. When I tried to knock it off the wall into a plastic bucket, it crawled up into the rafters. I climbed up after it and took a machete. If I couldn't catch it, I was at least not going to let it alive in the kid's bedroom. It tried to hide but I could see it and slaughtered it with the machete. We all slept better that night.

The largest centipede we saw was about 10 inches long but they could probably grow longer. They were poisonous and greatly feared.

We lived too far away from the Andes Mountains to be bothered by jaguars, wild pigs, monkeys and an assortment of other wildlife. There was an animal that the Colombians called a *zorro*. In Spanish, zorro means fox. I saw just three of them during my years in Colombia. This animal was a cat but had a face like a fox. It was coal black, about the size of a medium sized dog, and I never heard of one harming people. It was like a small black panther. It was too dry and hot where we lived for that kind of wildlife.

During the years we lived in Merachon, from 1967 to 1978, there was no guerrilla activity in our area. Guerrillas are illegal anti-government military rebel forces. The activity was confined to the lower parts of Colombia. We have heard rumors that in recent years, groups of guerrillas have moved into the Sierra Nevada mountain range and into the upper parts of the Guajira peninsula. The guerrillas are dangerous and have caused a lot of trouble for missionaries and Americans in general.

Stealing among the Colombians seemed to be a way of life. For that reason, the Colombian houses were fortified with barred windows and the better houses had barred doorways. Patios were enclosed by high walls with broken glass cemented on top, making it dangerous to crawl over. Thieves were armed with guns and knives. Knives were favored because they didn't make noise. It was the responsibility of the residents to protect themselves. Dogs were kept to sound the alarm if someone tried to break into a house. Sometimes it was best not to disturb a thief who succeeded in entering a house; playing opossum could save your life. One of the Colombian pastors lost his wife who awakened one night and discovered thieves on the premises. It is thought that she knew them so they killed her to keep from being identified.

Traveling on public transportation could be dangerous, mainly because so many vehicles were poorly maintained. In the Guajira, very few women drove vehicles, and I never saw a Wayuu woman drive. Driving fast is macho. I never heard of a law about drunk driving. I saw some bad scenes that were a result of driving drunk. Sometimes it was the roads that were so bad that they caused accidents. Once when Betty and I were driving to Riohacha, we took a road along the beach. We came to a bridge the government had built over a canal that led to the salt beds. Before going up the ramp to go over the bridge, I decided to check the condition of the bridge first. I was shocked to see the bridge was out. If we had driven up onto it, we would have dropped down into the canal which was flowing very rapidly. There is no doubt in my mind that we might not have been able to survive a plunge into the rapid flowing canal. When we went to Colombia in 1961 there were no paved roads in the peninsula. Much progress has been made over the years since then. There is now a very good paved highway that leads from the Colombian/Venezuelan border through Maicao, Riohacha all the way to Santa Marta. Many streets in the major towns have been paved and roads that once were dirt trails are now paved.

When we traveled we always trusted the Lord to take care of us, and what can we say? We have no doubt that the Lord watched over us day and night, through sunshine and rain, through conflict and peace. We give Him all the praise for being such a caring and trustworthy God. God did not give us the spirit of fear.

CHAPTER EIGHT

Personal Experiences

Trust in the Lord with all thine heart; and lean not unto thine own understanding. In all thy ways acknowledge Him, and He shall direct thy paths.
Proverbs 3:5-6

We hate the troubles that come into our lives, but sometimes troubles are good theology teachers. They teach us that the Lord is not only aware of our problems, but He is always there and ready to help in the time of need. This does not mean that He will bail us out of a difficulty every time, but He might just give us grace to bear our burden. How encouraging it is to have a problem that seemingly has no solution, but when the matter is committed to the Lord, something happens that nicely resolves it. It has been a learning experience that when I have committed all my ways unto Him, He has, without question, directed my paths. I have lost count the number of times I had what seemed like an insurmountable problem with no way out, and I prayed. The way things turned out, I knew it had to be the Lord's work. He always has the answer; the exact right answer. I can relate only a handful of such experiences but there are many more than space allows.

When we joined the Mission in 1958, Rev. G. Hunter Norwood, general director of the South America Indian Mission, asked us where we would like to serve. Our answer was, "wherever we are most needed". He suggested Colombia and we agreed. After all, I had read an article in the Amazon Valley Indian about an Indian in Colombia who asked for someone to come and teach him and his family about God, and I said if the Lord would open the door for us, that is where we would go. Colombia was a closed door country, meaning, they were not giving visas to missionaries to enter the country. As mentioned in previous chapters, twice our applications for visas were denied. We tried a third time and our visas were granted. The lesson we learned from this experience was that the Lord is in charge. He will open and close doors as He wishes. No man can prevent God from doing what He wants to do, when He wants to do it. It was evident to us that the Lord wanted us to go to Colombia. We were the first "new" missionaries to enter the country from our Mission in eighteen years. A few months before we arrived in Colombia, John and Janet Breman were transferred from Bolivia. It was up to the Corwins, the Bremans and the Myers to carry on the work that had begun back in 1934.

During the second half of our first term in Colombia we lived in the town of Uribia. Uribia was miles from everywhere, and it was connected to the towns of Manaure and Maicao by the poorest of dirt roads. The roads were more like trails in most places. No missionary had ever lived in Uribia and we were not well received, both as missionaries and as Americans. One day a tremendous racket hit the roof of our rented house. The neighborhood kids were throwing stones up on the tin roof. Some stones came over the roof and landed in the patio. We made our kids come in the house so they wouldn't get hit with a stone. Some stones didn't make it up on the roof and hit the side of the house. I rushed to the door and the kids took off running, but I recognized some of them. The stone throwing became a daily routine. The boys would throw stones when they went to school in the morning, and again when they went home at noon for lunch and the afternoon siesta time. When they went back to school around two o'clock in the afternoon, they would throw more stones, and again when they returned home later in the afternoon. Then for a diversion in the evening, they came back and threw more stones. The roof was suffering damage and we were afraid our kids would be hit by falling stones in the patio. I tried to talk to the boys about the problem and one of the boys hit me in the back with a stone. I gave up. One day a new friend, named Guillermo Estrada, came by the house for a visit. He had bought a Bible and had questions so we were having a Bible study. Suddenly, the stone throwing started and he was quite startled by the racket. He jumped up and ran to the door to see what was going on. I stayed put. He asked me why I wasn't coming to the door to see who was throwing stones, and I told him the practice had been going on for about three months, and everybody in town knew about it and thought it was funny. He suggested I go to the police station and make a complaint. He said the police would arrest the boys and take them to jail and their parents would have to pay a fine to get them out. I told him I could not do such a thing because I was trying to make friends in the town and having their boys arrested would only alienate the people further. I suggested that he and I try another approach; "let's pray about it, now, together". He may have recited prayers but was not a Christian so he never really prayed a believer's prayer a day in his life. He thought it was a novel idea and told me to go ahead and pray; he would listen. I prayed that, if the Lord so willed, He would intervene for us and stop the stone throwing. We went back to our Bible study, and then he left for home. A week later he came back with more questions and during our Bible study, he remembered the stone throwing. I told him that since the day we had prayed that the Lord would cause it to stop, only one little boy tried unsuccessfully to throw a stone up onto the roof. He leaned back in his chair with a grin on his face like the cat that swallowed the canary. "Do you know why the stone throwing stopped?" he asked. He told me he went to the houses of the culprits and told their parents about it. The parents were surprised and said they were unaware of it. One lady got a switch and thrashed her two boys for participating in the stone throwing. Others warned their boys to discontinue the practice. What could I say? I said, "All I know is that I had a serious problem, I prayed about it, and the stone throwing stopped. How the Lord chose to answer our prayer about it was up to Him." I thanked Guillermo for his interest and help. The stone throwing never resumed. Answered prayer helped me and him, also.

I mentioned before that Uribia did not have a public market. People had little stores in their houses. There was a place where cows, goats, sheep and pigs were killed. It was called the *matadero*. The man who did the butchering called himself *Negro Libre*, which means "free black". When I tried to buy meat from him, he held his razor sharp knife to my neck and told me there was no meat for me and never to come back. Later that year Betty and I came up with a plan to buy fifty calendars to pass out at Christmas time to those who had been friendly toward us. The calendars came and looked nice. We had our identity printed on them so the people could learn our names. I hid them in a bag and walked around town passing them out. I discovered that calendars were highly prized and hard to come by, so the people greatly appreciated them. When I arrived back home, I met a man in front of the house and we got into a conversation. I gave him one of the four calendars I had left. And while we were talking who should show up but Negro Libre. He butted rudely into our conversation so I backed off a couple steps. He complained about how hard it was to collect what people owed him and how so many tried to cheat him. As he was leaving, he looked at me and roughly asked what I was doing. I told him I was passing out calendars and offered him one. He took it, looked it over, thanked me for it, and told me he would be butchering the next morning. If I wanted meat, come around and he would save me some. I assured him I would be there. The next morning I showed up, and sure enough, he had saved me a filet mignon and some bones for soup. He appreciated that I had the exact change because most people came without any money. He had to make the rounds in the afternoon collecting what people owed him and more often than not it was like pulling hen's teeth. He became my friend. Who could have known that a simple thing like a calendar could change a person's attitude and make them open to the gospel? In our family devotions we had prayed for friends and for food. In the most gracious way, the Lord answered our prayers. The Bible says that the Lord has invited us to "make our requests and petitions known unto the Lord." Philippians 4:6. What a wonderful resource He is.

The most important item a person possesses in Colombia is the "*cedula*". Every person must have one and it must be carried on a person at all times outside the house. One day while traveling from Carraipia to Fonseca with a little boy from our church, I knew we were coming to a check point along the road where authorities check documents. I had been there many times over the years. I reached for my wallet in which I carried my cedula and – no wallet. I knew I had it when we boarded the bus. I began a frantic search through all my pockets – no cedula. My friend and I looked around the seat, on the floor, every nook and cranny where it could have fallen – no cedula. I explained to my friend the problem I was going to have, that I would be arrested and he would have to go back to Carraipia and explain to Betty what happened. We took a moment to pray and we asked the Lord to help us. I decided to take one more look. We looked every place we had looked before. We lifted up the bench seat and – there was the cedula. I was totally surprised and my heart was filled with gratitude that the Lord had helped us. Since we had looked in that very spot before, I cannot to this day explain why we didn't see it the first time. We continued on our journey to Fonseca discussing how the Lord answers prayer. He specializes in answering our prayers. Every answered prayer encourages our hearts in knowing that our God is a real, living God who has an interest in our daily lives and problems.

Some things seem so small that it seems silly to pray about them. Evidently, God is of a different opinion. When we were having our house built in Merachon, I was also preaching at the two churches in Carraipia and Maicao. When I was free, I would travel about sixty miles out to the building site transporting workers and supplies. On one trip, after it had rained some, we came to a long mud hole and got a little stuck. With a little pushing, we unstuck the Jeep and continued on our way. Then the Jeep started to cough and sputter, and finally it died. I put the hood up and I saw that gasoline was dripping from the carburetor. I had no idea what was wrong or how to fix it, but I couldn't just stand there, so I took the carburetor off, took it apart and made an adjustment that I later learned was exactly the right thing to do, and commenced to install the carburetor back on the Jeep. I mentioned to the fellows with me that I wanted to be very careful not to drop the little screw that held the linkage to the carburetor. You guessed it; I dropped it. "No problem", I said. "We'll just push the Jeep back a few feet and we would see a little dimple in the sand where the screw fell." We pushed the Jeep back about six feet. I looked and saw maybe a hundred dimples. We began carefully sifting through the sand and we could not find the screw. We looked and looked. I thought perhaps it never fell as far as the sand, so checked the Jeep, but to no avail. We were becoming discouraged as we continued looking. Time was of the essence. We had to have that screw. One of the men said he had a solution. "Let's pray about it", he suggested. And we did. We asked the Lord to help us find the screw. Amen! We began to search again and within ten seconds I was holding that little, all important screw in my hand. This time, I took great care in putting it where it belonged and we continued on our way without further incident. This missionary listened to a lecture from his traveling companions about how the Lord answers prayer, no matter how small and simple or how huge and complicated, it's all the same to Him. He's the Master of it all.

After we had lived in Merachon for several years, I was invited to go with a family to the Alta Guajira where they had family they wanted to visit. I think I was invited because I had a Jeep and could provide transportation, but I was glad for the opportunity to expand my horizons. The Alta Guajira is the northern end of the peninsula. We made the trip, which took about seven hours, and I noticed that as we neared our destination, the brakes were getting spongy. I never traveled without a can or two of brake fluid. I added some brake fluid and the brakes were fine, but only for a short time. When we arrived at our destination, and formalities were over, I took a moment to check the brakes. I discovered to my dismay that a nipple by which the brakes are bled had broken off. A rock must have bounced up and hit it. I had no idea how to fix it. I would have to drive all the way back home without brakes. We stayed overnight and left the next day for home, traveling very carefully. At one point along the way we came to an area with small hills, a rocky area where I could not see the road ahead very well. As we rounded a curve around some rocks and started down a small hill, we met a caravan of Wayuu coming up with their donkeys loaded with water jars and people. I had no brakes and plowed through them as they desperately tried to get off the road. How I got through them without hitting anyone is a miracle. If I had hit one of them, it would probably have been the end of our missionary career. They would have hunted me down until they found me and probably killed me. Had we tried to stop, which I couldn't without brakes, they may have done us harm then and there. I praise the Lord for sparing us and preventing a major disaster. It was an instant answer to prayer before we had a chance to pray, but we prayed afterwards and thanked the Lord for protecting the Wayuu and us.

I went to Maicao shopping one day and as I was crossing the plaza, I noticed a large crowd of Wayuu down a side street. That usually meant a fight, and I never went near them. Since the crowd was quiet, curiosity got the best of me and I went to see what interested the Wayuu so much. They were gathered around a man who was selling an ointment which he claimed would protect a person from poisonous snake bites when it was rubbed on the legs. One peso, about ten cents in American money, for a little tin. The man proceeded to prove his point. Out of a large crate he produced the largest rattlesnake I had ever seen. It had to be a minimum of six feet long. He very carefully picked it up, and holding it by the head walked around showing the crowd its fangs which dripped with venom when tapped. He pried its mouth open and it was cavernous. What a sight! Since he had rubbed the ointment on his hands and other parts, the snake would not bite him, of course. Many Colombians had joined the crowd of Wayuu and the man sold little tins of ointment as fast as he could open the boxes. He had laid the rattlesnake on the pavement and it crawled about the small crates he had stacked around, seemingly not interested in anybody. I noticed there was a cupboard standing upright on legs about three feet high. The cupboard (for lack of a better name) was about thirty inches across and thirty inches high and about twelve inches deep. It had two front doors and the box was painted a gaudy green. When the ointment was sold, he walked over to the cupboard and opened the doors. Inside was a shelf and to my astonishment there was a girl's head resting on a shelf. I thought at first it must be a wax model of a head, but that was quickly dispelled when he spoke to the girl and she answered him. He asked her name and she gave it – Maria. The shelf was about ten inches high. I wondered where the rest of the girl's body was as there was very little space under the shelf for a body, no matter how small. I walked up close to study the girl's head and she looked directly at me. It gave me the chills and I backed away. The man said Maria was twelve years old and could tell fortunes. He closed the cupboard doors and opened them as fast as he closed them. The girl's head was gone. I got as close as I could and looked into the hole on the shelf and could see nothing but darkness. I wondered, where was the head and body? He closed the doors and opened them and there was the girl's head. I asked myself how she could disappear and appear so fast! He closed the doors again and walked through the crowd and asked the girl if he was touching a man or a woman, and she would give the correct answer. Then he asked the color of the shirt of the man he was touching, and she would give the color. He asked a couple more questions and from inside the cupboard with the doors closed, she would give the correct answers. I knew this was all coded so there was nothing mysterious about that. What was mysterious was the girl. How could she have jammed her body underneath the shelf on which her head rested? I never learned the answer, but a year later I was walking through the park in the same town and passed a tent set up in the Plaza. In front was a sign to come in and see the girl who had no limbs, just a small body. The fee was five pesos to go in. I did not go in to see if this was the same girl, but if I were a gambling man, I'd bet a dollar it was. I have no doubt demons were at work deceiving the gullible. Satan and his associates are good at that. We must always be on prayer guard against the wiles of the devil, especially in spiritual matters.

An amazing answer to prayer happened in 1977. The whole family needed new Colombian visas in our passports. I invited our field director,

Bob Crump, to accompany me to Bogota, where I planned to apply for the visas. When we arrived in Bogota we went to the office where visas are granted. We arrived about the time the office was opening and a crowd was forming. Everyone was clamoring for attention, waving papers, pushing and shoving. We were in back of the crowd and nobody paid attention to us. That is, nobody but the office boy. It was his duty to sharpen pencils, serve coffee to the employees in the office, empty waste baskets and run errands. He appeared at a side door down the hall and beckoned for us to approach him. He asked us what we wanted, and I explained the matter of the visas. He advised us to come back in the morning around nine o'clock and he would take us in to meet the person who could grant us visas. Bob and I remarked to each other that the office boy who waits on everyone else is going to take us into the inner office with this highly important mission? We thought he was just trying to look important. What could we do? We felt that we had no recourse but to take this boy at his word and see what happens. Bob and I went to the office the next morning at the appointed time. At first the office boy paid no attention to us. Getting visas had been a matter of prayer. They were absolutely necessary for us to stay in Colombia. The crowd was the same as the day before, hollering to be waited on, waving papers, pushing and shoving. We waited at the back of the crowd. The office boy saw us but did nothing which did not surprise us. A half hour went by and the boy appeared at the door down the hall and motioned for us to come. He told us he had given our information to the secretary of the person who grants visas, and then to our complete amazement, conducted us into the secretary's office. He introduced us to a very cultured young secretary who invited us to sit down and ordered coffee for us. She told us that Dona Clara had not yet arrived at the office, and when she did, we could have an audience with her. We had a lengthy conversation with the secretary and she wanted to know all about us and our work. The person who could grant us visas was a lady who, we would learn momentarily, was very aristocratic, beautiful and educated. When she arrived, within minutes we were escorted into her office by her secretary. Dona Clara invited us to be seated. We did what all courteous Colombians do; we sat down and engaged in small talk and conversation before getting down to business. When she learned that I needed our visas renewed in our family passports, she took our passports and looked through them, making comments and asking questions as she went. When she was satisfied that our passports were in order, she said she could see no reason why we could not have them granted. She called a young man into her office, ordered him to put visas in each passport and to have it all done by two o'clock in the afternoon. The man looked surprised which told us this was not usual procedure. Bob and I left the office knowing that the Lord had taken care of an important matter, which to us meant He wanted us in Colombia for a while longer. That afternoon at two o'clock, we went to the office to pick up our passports. As they were handed to us, the officer in charge told us she had worked there for twenty years and had never seen this done before. It usually took days to get all this done. We thanked her for her kindness and left the office praising the Lord for His wonderful provision for us. As I write these lines, I am still praising the Lord for what He did for us, and how He did it. He gave us first class attention. It has been incidents like this that have caused us as believers to trust Him all the more and to realize that He is not a passive God who just sits somewhere in the heavens above watching the world scene. He takes a practical part in our lives. He is a wonder working God.

I cannot tell you how many times I questioned my presence in Colombia. Things happened that raised questions in my mind. There was the time when we were living in Carraipia and I was serving as pastor of two churches, one in the town and another in Maicao, which was several miles away. On a day that was going to be especially busy, I ate breakfast, rushed out the door and got into my Jeep. When I turned the ignition key, all I got was a sick whirring sound and the engine would not turn over. I tried again, and a third time with the same results. I got out, raised the hood, and stared at the engine. Truly, I did not know what I was looking at. I had no mechanical skills. I reasoned that if the Jeep would not start, the problem must be with the starter. I took the starter off and took it into the house. With great care, drawing a diagram on the floor with chalk as I disassembled it, I cleaned every part until they shined like new. I put it all together, following the diagram on the floor, installed it on the Jeep, turned the ignition key, and all I got was the same sickening whirring sound. Whoops! I must have missed something. I went through the whole procedure again, paying special attention to each part, looking for something I must have missed the first time. When I was satisfied that I had done my best, I assembled the starter and put it back on the Jeep. The engine whined and would not turn over. I took the starter off a third time, took it all apart, and suddenly came to my senses. With the parts scattered on the floor, I realized I had no idea what I was doing. I gave up and sat in a rocker, looking at the mess of parts on the floor. I had a pity party. "What am I doing?" I asked myself, reminding me that I knew nothing about mechanics. I didn't know what I was doing. Why was I even in Colombia? Missionaries need to be the jack of all trades and at least the master of something. I couldn't think of one thing of which I was the master. I couldn't fix things. I couldn't build things. I couldn't even build a box. I was painfully aware that I couldn't even speak Spanish well. I was deficient in everything. Why was I here? Then two wonderful things happened that are impossible to forget.

The first thing was that I was suddenly overcome with a flood of assurance that I was exactly where the Lord wanted me to be, at the time He wanted me to be there, doing exactly what He wanted me to do. With that settled, I prayed, "Lord, You will have to help me with this problem. I don't know what I'm doing. I'm counting on You to help me with the Jeep problem." And just then the second thing happened. I was right about my shortcomings. A missionary ought to be the jack of all trades and at least the master of something, because so often there is no one else to turn to for help. Every missionary should learn to speak the language of the native speakers as fluently and correctly as possible. I certainly came up short in that department.

I heard a vehicle pull up and stop in front of the house. I opened the door and there was my coworker, John Breman. He lived in Fonseca, three hours away, and John was a first rate auto mechanic. Was this how the Lord was going to answer my prayer and solve my problem? John had a friend with him and they had a problem and needed some help. They came in and sat down, and after a lengthy discussion, I assured John that I could help them. John barely glanced at the starter motor parts on the floor. After some brief small talk, they got up to leave and John asked me why I had the starter apart. I explained that the Jeep wouldn't start. We went out to look at the Jeep, and after a minute or two, he announced that there was nothing wrong with anything. "Maybe a little dirt." He advised me to take every electrical wire off and clean it until it shinned, one wire at a time. "Put the starter back on the Jeep and it will start." And John and his friend left. So, I did as John said. I cleaned the connections of every wire, plus the battery posts and cables. I got in and turned the ignition and Varoooom! The Jeep roared to life and I never had another problem with dirty cables and wires. Just think of the timing. John could have come any day of the week, but he came at exactly the right time, when I had prayed about the matter, and John gave me exactly the right advice. Does the Lord hear and answer our prayers? Nobody will ever convince me that He doesn't.

One of the difficult issues I had to deal with was that of crossing the Colombian-Venezuelan border. The first time I made such a trip into Venezuela, I had an experience that left a deep impression on my mind. The Wayuu did not need documents to go back and forth, but everyone else did. Though the Colombians and Venezuelans needed passports and visas, they didn't bother with either. They just paid a "fine" for not having them. In cash, of course. In English, "fine" is spelled "bribe", but that is a nasty word so we'll not use it. There are certain towns, called free port towns, along the border that one can cross into without the need for documents, and Maicao is one of them. Passports were expensive, and visas hard to get, to say nothing of the time it took to get them. When I went to Venezuela the first time, I

98

had all the proper documents required. So rare was it that somebody would show up at the border with them that when I presented them to the border guards, they didn't even know what they were. They got together in a huddle to discuss what to do about the matter, and came up with a document they said I was missing, so I would have to pay a "fine". The document requested was a health certificate. I remembered I had an international health certificate with me and presented it to them. They were quite surprised. Another huddle. I did not have the right kind of health certificate. What I had was an international certificate and they wanted a Colombian health certificate. In fact, I was very sure there was no such thing, so what could I do. They were not about to let me cross the border without paying a "fine". I was expected to attend a very important meeting in Maracaibo, Venezuela. Instead of paying the "fine", I consulted a higher authority; I prayed and asked the Lord to help me do the right thing. He didn't let me down. After I prayed about the matter, a vehicle pulled up and out stepped important looking uniformed men, obviously officials of the border guards, but higher in authority. There was a lot of loud talking, barking orders, rustling of papers, scurrying around and questions. They were just checking the situation at the border. The man who seemed to be in charge happened to spy me standing by the side of the road with papers in my hand, and demanded of the guards as to who I was and what I wanted. They said I was there crossing the border. The officer walked over, took the papers from my hand, looked them over and said loudly, "he has all the right documents, in perfect order," and demanded to know why I was left standing there. In less time than it takes to tell, the border guards took my papers and passport, stamped the necessary entries in them, and I caught the next vehicle headed for Maracaibo. Let me repeat; I was on an important mission, I had a problem I could not solve, I prayed about it, and the Lord was right there helping me get exactly what I needed, doing it at the right time and in the proper way.

There was one detail which I had not checked. My visa was to expire in four days and I expected to be in Venezuela about five or six days. The visit was to check out the school in Rubio, Venezuela for our children. I made it to Maracaibo in time for the meeting with the school board of the Evangelical Alliance Mission that operated the school for missionary children. The day after the meeting, I went with some of the board members to Rubio to see the school and meet some of the personnel. I was impressed by the good roads in Venezuela and by the school, a day's drive from Maracaibo. After a few days, I headed back to Maracaibo and Colombia. The trip was not without problems. First, I bought a bus ticket the day before leaving, and early the next morning I went to the bus station to catch the bus. The driver refused to let me on. I insisted I had a ticket, but he insisted the bus was full and there was no room for me. He closed the door and took off, leaving me high and dry at the bus station. I had to stay an extra day and try again the next morning and this time with success. But the bus I was on only went half way to Maracaibo. I got off the bus, grabbed my little suitcase, and looked for transportation headed for Maracaibo. There were no buses, but I found a car that made trips back and forth every day, so I hitched a ride and was in Maracaibo in a couple hours. I then caught a taxi headed for the border and rode for another couple hours, arriving at the Venezuelan-Colombian border around five o'clock on a Friday afternoon. I checked out of Venezuela. There is a no man's land of two or three miles between the two border posts. When I arrived at the Colombian border, I was informed by the guard that my visa had expired and I could not enter the country. I checked the visa in my passport and he was right. Now I really had a problem. I could not go back to Venezuela because I had already checked out. I had no documents that would allow me back into Venezuela. It would not have helped to return anyhow because there was nothing I could do until offices opened on Monday. I did not have enough money to stay at a hotel until Monday and did not know how long it would take to get a tourist visa to enter Colombia. That could take days. I explained my situation to the border guard. He couldn't have cared less and said so. I stood around for a half hour and very little traffic passed by in either direction. The guard was there by himself and brought out an empty pop bottle case for me to sit on. I sat and I prayed. "Lord, I don't know what to do. I need your help once again. Please help me to do the right thing and be a witness for You." I knew if I paid a "fine", the guard would have stamped me into the country, but that is not the right thing to do. Soon the guard brought out a chair and leaned it against the wall beside me and we talked. He asked me where I was going and was surprised when I told him where I lived and that we had a mission work among the Indians. He had more questions than I can remember, but seemed to be impressed with what we were doing in Merachon. When the conversation ended and there was a silence between us, he asked for my passport again. He went into his little office, and I heard him bang, bang, bang, stamping my documents. He came out and handed them to me and said, "The next time you leave the country, make sure your documents are in order." I thanked him kindly and when the next vehicle passed by, I got a ride into Maicao. I paid no fine, but I had an opportunity to share the gospel with a young man who may never have heard it before. I had a problem and it was serious. I prayed and asked the Lord for His help. He did not let me down. The Lord proved to me once again that He was reliable.

As mentioned in a previous chapter, the *cedula* was a very important document that must be carried for identification at all times. Betty and I

100

were in the city of Barranquilla on business and were about to head for home in the Guajira. We boarded a bus in the late afternoon and had about a half hour to wait before leaving. I got off the bus to run a quick errand and on the way back to the bus I had my pocket picked. I had always thought that I would be able to feel somebody putting their hands into my pockets, but this experience proved me wrong. Some Colombians are the best pick pockets in the world. They have what is called the "jingle bells school" in which they set up a dummy with bells on it and pockets. They practice picking pockets until they can do it without ringing the bells.

As I was walking back to the bus I saw four young men coming down the sidewalk toward me and knew immediately what they were doing. They must have been graduates of the "jingle bells school". They fanned out across the sidewalk and pretended to be trying to pass people, but in reality they were pressing people into a small crowd and one or two of the men went through the crowd quickly and picked pockets. I pressed my back against the wall but they got behind me and pushed me out and quickly went on their way. I thought they at least did not get my wallet, but when I checked, it was gone, cedula and all. There was very little cash in the wallet, but it was my cedula I was concerned about. I knew that the bus would be stopped two or three times and everyone would be checked before we got home. I envisioned myself being arrested, an American without identification, at a time when Americans were heavily involved in drug traffic. I had no way of proving who I was or what I was doing in the country. I tried to find the four young men and demand my wallet back, but they seemed to have disappeared into thin air. I boarded the bus and told Betty what happened, what we might expect and what she would have to do (like visit me in prison). When the bus pulled out and headed for the Guajira, I was praying hard and asked the Lord to intervene for me. He did. When we travelled to Barranquilla a day earlier, we were stopped at a *reten* (a road block) at least three different locations and checked. I knew that on the way home we would be stopped at these same places. When we came to the first reten, it was closed and we went on through without being stopped. The same happened at the second reten. When we came to the third, it was a reten maintained by the Colombian army and they were out in full force. All the men were ordered off the bus and everybody's identity was being checked. The commander was there when we passed on the way to town and he and I had a brief but good conversation as he personally checked my cedula. He was there again on the way home and remembered me and just motioned me to board the bus without asking for my cedula. I made it home without being checked once. But that's not the end of the story.

Two days after arriving home we went to Riohacha so I could go into DAS and tell them I had my pocket picked and lost my cedula. When we

101

arrived in town, we went first to the home of missionaries, Bob and Helen Crump, and had a cup of good Colombian coffee. Before I got up to go down to the office, Bob said he had something for me. He handed me my wallet. I cannot tell you how very surprised I was. He explained that they, too, had been in Barranquilla the day before and passed by the Mission bookstore in downtown Barranquilla. Jack Hough, who ran the bookstore along with his wife Bea, handed him my wallet. Four young men brought it in and asked if Hough's knew the owner of the wallet. Jack gave them two hundred pesos for it and passed the wallet on to Crumps who in turn passed it on to one very relieved missionary whose prayers had been answered once again. I gladly reimbursed and thanked Jack Hough the next time I saw him. I cannot count the number of times I have had problems I could not solve, and the Lord bailed me out. He has invited us to let our petitions and requests be made know unto Him, Philippians 4:6. I praise the Lord for this gracious invitation. I took Him up on it many times. We know and serve a God who never disappoints us and always keeps his promises.

CHAPTER NINE

A School for the Wayuu

For whatsoever things were written aforetime were written for our learning, that we through patience and comfort of the scriptures might have hope.

Romans 15:4

When we moved from the town of Carraipia to Merachon to live among the Wayuu, one of the first things we did was have a school house built for the Wayuu children. If they were ever going to be saved and established in the faith, they would have to know how to read. If a church could be established among them, they would have to know how to read the Scriptures for themselves. Once we were settled in our house, our first order of business was to have the Indians build us a school house that was like their own houses, except that it would have a cement floor. The adult Wayuu were not enthusiastic about this project. Our goal was to teach the children to read Spanish because, at that time, their own language was not yet reduced to writing. The Summer Institute of Linguistics was working on it but, at that time, it was going to be several years before they produced a Bible in the Wayuu language. There was already a Spanish edition of the Bible, so this was a provision until a Bible in the Wayuu language, called Wayuuniki, was available.

The Indians went to work and cut the poles for the walls. They cut the sticks that would be nailed to the walls, inside and out. I hauled the poles to the building site. They dug the holes for the poles and the walls went up. They dug the adobe dirt that would become the mud for the walls. I hauled the water to make the mud. They cut the thatch for the roof from cactus plants. The building went up rather quickly. I paid them for their labor and they were satisfied and pleased to have some income. The day after the mud was mixed, the Wayuu Indians gathered at the building site and began making balls of mud which they placed in the cavity of the walls. When the walls were filled, they then covered them inside and out with a layer of mud to hide the sticks and make a smooth wall. I made four windows and a door which I installed. I had two of the Wayuu men help me lay a cement floor. They had never done anything like that before, so with my help and instructions, we laid a very level smooth floor. This was a new experience for them. When the building was completely finished, we were ready for business. I hung a large homemade black board on the wall, and made two simple but sturdy tables and benches for inside. Finally, I hung a heavy

Two Wayuu men helping with the construction of the first Wayuu school building.

Our first students standing in front of our school building before it was plastered.

Ruthie sitting in front of the finished mud school building after it was plastered on the outside. It had a thatch roof and cement floor inside.

piece of broken spring from a bull dozer from a nearby tree. That was our bell. We sent out word about when our school would open. Five Wayuu children came, all girls.

The ages of the five girls were about seven to sixteen. The first year of school, everybody was in first grade. Since the Wayuu did not know how old they were, we decided to check their teeth. If they were not yet missing any baby teeth, they were too young to attend. They had to be missing at least two baby teeth, which we figured made them about six or seven years old.

The first class of the morning was Bible reading from the Spanish Bible. Since they couldn't read yet, I did the reading. Then we had a time of prayer. Since none of them were believers, I did the praying, too. The second class was learning the Spanish alphabet, both how to write the letters and how to say them. We combined vowels and consonants and slowly built a vocabulary. They learned quickly. The third class of the morning was numbers. We taught them to count in Spanish, and the denominations of Colombian money. This was something that they seemed to already know. Many Wayuu did not know a five peso bill from a fifty peso bill. I once saw a merchant take a fifty peso bill from a Wayuu man for something purchased, convincing him it was a five peso bill. The man didn't know the difference. We also taught the Wayuu weights and measures.

One class day during the first year, I was showing them how to put vowels and consonants together and formed a couple Wayuu words. I did not tell them I was making Wayuu words on the blackboard. I wrote "ama". Suddenly, one girl exclaimed, "that's our word for horse." The class was surprised that words from their language could be written down. The children were smart and caught on quickly.

The first year closed for vacation and it proved to be a successful year. After a three month break, the second year of school began. Now we had a second grade and a new set of first graders. The first grade students went through the same program as the second graders did the year before. But the second grade students were now able to read quite a bit. We included some little books about history and geography that are used in the Colombian schools. We made them pay for their books, charging them a subsidized price so it would be affordable, and they did not object. They liked being able to read the books in Spanish and know what they were reading. They would take the books home and read them to the adults in Spanish and explain to them the meaning in Wayuunaiki. Another thing we did in second grade, since they could read fairly well, was have them do the Bible reading instead of me doing it. So they read the Bible, each taking a turn each day, and I did the praying. We had another good school year.

The third year we had to add a class in the early afternoon to accommodate the third grade class. Grades one and two were held in the morning. This time, they not only read the Bible, but I taught them to pray. "Who wants to pray first?" I asked. These students were not yet believers in the Lord and had never prayed. They looked at each other and finally one girl said she would pray. She started out in her own language, "Tata, Maregua, majusu taya." (Translated "Father God, I am bad." in English). I will never forget it. I don't remember the rest of her prayer, but it broke the ice, and after that, they took turns praying.

Finally, we added a fourth class. By this time, our children were heading for boarding school in Venezuela, so Betty, not having our own children to teach, took over the Wayuu school. The children loved her. Betty enjoyed the time with the Wayuu children and developed good rapport with them. It was good for her, too, because it helped her learn the Indian language even more. The girls liked coming to school because it got them out of work, too, like going to the windmill to wash clothing and hauling water back to the house, or collecting firewood. The boys liked coming to school because it got them out of work, like tending the sheep, or taking the goats to the windmill. School was conducted nine months a year, but just four days a week. On Friday, we went to Maicao to do our shopping. Saturday we rested and prepared for Sunday. I checked over the Jeep or truck every Saturday to make sure it was land-worthy and would take us for services in Manaure and/or Uribia without trouble.

The Wayuu school was conducted all eleven years we lived in Merachon, and the result was that it produced many bilingual Wayuu who know Spanish, many of them better than I ever did. Today, as this book goes to print, the Summer Institute of Linguistics has reduced the Wayuu language to writing and translated the Scriptures for them. They have the Word of God in their own language which was dedicated in 2002 in Uribia.

After we left Colombia in 1978, one of the boys who grew up in our school became the pastor of the Wayuu in that particular area. He also had a school of his own and was the children's teacher. The Colombian government named him the health coordinator for the Wayuu in the area. He was instrumental in leading many of the adults in his extensive family to the Lord. He conducted evangelistic work among the many Wayuu rancherias where he lived.

The Indians were quick to learn other things, too. Our children taught them how to play checkers. Many days after school, they would congregate in the front room of our house and set up the checker boards. We had about ten of them. They pared off and had a great time.

One summer we had three college students come and stay with us a few weeks. They came to help me with some of the manual labor around the place, including drilling a well. They came into the house one afternoon for water and a rest and saw the Wayuu children playing checkers. This surprised them and they watched to see how the Wayuu children played. One of the college boys informed us that he was the checker champion at his college. After watching for several minutes, he said he wanted to play one of the Wayuu kids. A young girl, about eight years old, was standing there and did not have a partner to play with, so she was only too happy to have a game with the "college student." She started first, zip. He made a carefully calculated move. Her turn, zip. He made another well reasoned out move. Her turn, zip. She beat him. He was a little embarrassed and wanted a rematch, announcing that this time he would be more careful and take her more seriously. He lost that game, too, and the third, and the fourth and the fifth. After losing seventeen games in a row without a win, he slowly stood up and said, "Boy, somebody sure taught these kids to play good!"

Our kids taught the Wayuu how to play ball, with a rubber ball, of course. The Wayuu loved it and after school many of the kids would pick sides and we would have a rip snorting ball game in front of our house. Connie James, a single missionary, came to live on our station for a year. She taught first and second grade. She also got involved in the ball games. When somebody was "out", she used the English word for "out". The Wayuu did not know what she was saying, but "out" sounds nearly like the Wayuu word for "dead", "oktushii", so that became the word for "out". If you were "out", you were "dead".

On one occasion when school was over for the day, some men from the States were visiting at our house and noticed that the boys had sling shots in their belts. They asked if the boys were any good with their sling shots. I assured them that they were quite accurate, so they challenged the boys. A peso for every can they knocked over. A row of cans were set up and the boys were licking their chops. I was hoping the men had enough pesos in their pockets. The boys eagerly lined up for turns at the cans. In less time than it takes to tell, the boys cleaned the men out of all the one peso bills they had, and it didn't take long to do it. The men enjoyed the entertainment and admired the skill shown by the Wayuu boys. The boys enjoyed demonstrating their skills and going home with some pesos in their pockets.

The purpose of the school was to teach the Wayuu children and young people to read Spanish so they could read the Bible for themselves. This was a temporary arrangement because the Summer Institute of Linguistics was hard at work producing a Bible in the Wayuu language. The program worked. Betty and I left Colombia for good in 1978 and I did not return until the spring of 2002, nearly twenty five years later. I was amazed to see how the work had grown, especially under the leadership of one of our former school students, Jaime Enrique Epineyu. He was their pastor, school teacher as well as the chief of his extended family. I spent three days living with the Wayuu, sleeping at night under the stars in a hammock, and receiving many visitors who knew me from the years we lived in Merachon. Many of the visitors were former students. My, how they had grown up and changed! Most were married with families. I was surprised and saddened to learn of the number of Wayuu we had known who had died. One of their chief enemies was tuberculosis. Some who had died were our former students and others were their parents or family members. It was a great joy to learn that many of them had come to know the Lord through Jaime who was their pastor.

Lest it be thought that Betty and I were the only missionaries from our mission who worked with the Wayuu, credit must be given to another couple, Winfield and Francis Buckman. They also worked with the Wayuu. The Buckmans lived in Maicao and their house became a center for the Wayuu work. When the Wayuu went to town, they would go to the Buckman's residence for an assortment of reasons. Mainly, it was a place to gather, rest, get a drink of water, and store things they were buying to take back home later in the day. The Buckmans had a school for the Wayuu youth in their garage area. This school produced some of the most dedicated young pastors the Wayuu work enjoys today. They were a dedicated couple who worked tirelessly and the Wayuu had a great love and respect for them. Both Winfield, who was known as Buck to everyone, and Frances are now with the Lord awaiting the meeting at the Bema seat (reward seat) of Christ where they will receive a well deserved crown for their labor.

Not all the indigenous people the South America Mission worked with in Colombia were Wayuu. Bob and Ruth Ann Moyer lived and worked among the Indians in the Sierra Nevada mountain range. There were two main tribes, namely, the Kogi and the Arawak who lived there. Work with Indians is difficult because they are slow to respond to the preaching of the Gospel of Christ. Many times missionaries went to indigenous tribes, trying to reach them from the nearby Colombian towns. What happened was that the Colombians responded much more quickly than the Indians, and soon there would be a group of Colombian believers to work with, and the Indians would be left untended. That is why Betty and I decided to live out among the Wayuu instead of living in a town which would have been more convenient.

Language is always a barrier to progress. It seems that there was always one child in our school who knew enough Spanish to help the others learn what we were teaching. The Wayuu have their own style of music, so teaching them hymns and chorus's was interesting. They liked to sing, and picked up the songs in Spanish quickly. One night, after the family had gone to bed, I was lying awake for some reason. Some nights were too warm to sleep. I was resting in a hammock outside the house. From the nearest Wayuu houses, I could hear a little Wayuu boy singing Cristo Me Ama, (Jesus Loves Me in Spanish.) It truly was music to my ears. That little Wayuu boy is the same one who grew up in our school, attended our church services, and eventually became the Wayuu pastor for that area. He could tell his own people in two languages that the Lord Jesus loves them.

Some of the Wayuu who came for Sunday Services.

This photo was taken in 1968 after a Sunday service. This is in front of school/church building before it was plastered. Jaime is in the front with a cap.

CHAPTER TEN

Modes and Manners of Travel

Some trust in chariots, and some in horses, but we will remember the name of the Lord our God.　　　　　　　　　　　　　　　　　　　*Psalm 20:7*

Americans have transportation. Even high school students in their teens have their own cars and pickup trucks. People seem to be able to go anywhere, anytime, by any means of transportation. Americans can go from the beach to the moon. In so many other countries of the world, transportation is limited. There are places where the only mode of travel is the good ol' "shoe leather express". In other words, people walk everywhere. In Colombia I have traveled by plane, train, Jeep, bus, horse, mule, bicycle and an assortment of trucks. Many of those trips are memorable.

My first ride in Colombia was from the airport to the Genova hotel in Barranquilla when we first arrived in February of 1961. There was nothing unusual about the taxi. The driver was friendly. The paved streets were not bad. I could not help but notice that many of the cars on the road were old timers. There were many trucks and buses. After three days in Barranquilla, we headed back to the airport to travel by plane up into the Guajira peninsula where we would live for the next seventeen years. The plane was a DC-3 that carried about thirty five passengers, and may have been built before World War II. In my opinion, for what it's worth, the DC-3 is one of the most reliable airplanes ever built. They were used for many years after we arrived in the country and one trip in particular will forever live in my mind. In 1969 I was traveling from Maicao to Barranquilla, and for some reason, instead of taking the route along the seacoast, the pilot decided to fly around and through the eastern side of the Sierra Nevada Mountains. We flew through valleys where we could look at the sides of the mountains that were much higher than our plane. We could look straight across at people on the sides of the mountains who waved as we flew by. They were as high as we were. The wind currents were so strong that the plane just "crashed" through the wind, bucking and bouncing violently. What kept the wings intact, I'll never know. It made a believer out of me in the integrity of the DC-3. Everybody on board but me was sick and throwing up. Barf bags were exhausted quickly so people just threw up on the floor. Even a pig someone was carrying was sick, going at both ends. The stench was powerful enough to gag a maggot. I cannot say why I did not join the ranks of the sick. Once we were through the mountain passes, things calmed down and in another half hour we were landing in Barranquilla, much to everyone's relief.

On another occasion I was traveling to Bogota on a much larger four engine national airline plane. About a half hour before landing, I felt a bump, like the plane had run over a big rock. Since there are no rocks at twenty five thousand feet, it had me wondering. A few minutes after the bump, I looked out the window and could see that one engine was not running. The propeller was stationary. The pilot had shut down the engine. I was sitting in the middle of three seats. My field director, Bob Crump, was in the aisle seat, and next to the window was a cultured young lady who was an artist. I had been conversing with her and knew she had not noticed the engine. I told Bob that we better not mention it to her or she might panic. Curiosity got the best of us and I told her to look out the window. She did but did not notice the engine. I pointed out to her that the engine was not running. She panicked. She grabbed hold of me and frantically asked if we were going to crash. We assured her that we would land safely, which we did, much to her relief. Bob Crump never tired of kidding me about that flight to Bogota.

The plane flight most memorable of all took place when the parents of the children who were at the school in Rubio were traveling to Venezuela to pick them up for vacation. There were the Lees, Messers, Powels, Moyers and Betty and I; five families. We traveled from Valledupar to the city of Bucaramanga by bus. These were Blue Bird buses just like school buses here in the States. It was an overnight trip and part of the travel was over dusty dirt roads. Leaving Valledupar around four o'clock in the afternoon, we would arrive in Bucaramanga around seven o'clock or so the next morning. From Bucaramanga we traveled by car to Cucuta, a pretty city on the Colombian-Venezuelan border. From Cucuta we crossed the border into Venezuela, which was always a trying experience about which we all petitioned the Lord. On one particular trip we decided to fly from Bucaramanga to Cucuta. By car it was a five hour trip; by plane about twenty minutes. We bought our tickets, went to the airport on top of a mountain, and boarded a plane about the size of a DC-3, carrying about 30 passengers. The plane took off, circled for altitude and then flew over the high peaks of the Andes and down into Cucuta on the other side. As we reached our highest altitude, Betty asked me to feel the walls of the plane. We were seated over the wing. The inside walls were hot and the air in the plane was especially hot. She felt lightheaded and the stewardess gave her some rubbing alcohol to rub on her face. We landed and went about our business. The next day, that same airplane, making that same flight, flying over the Andes mountain peaks, lost both wings and went down into the forested east side of the mountains, leaving no survivors. They never did locate one of the wings. It was sobering to us all to think that we missed going on to glory by one day, and leaving at least sixteen children orphaned. A retired airline pilot explained to me that the Colombian airline used some of their best pilots to fly routes going into Cucuta because the updrafts crossing over the mountains were so strong. It took experienced pilots to safely fly those routes. He said the wings and fuselage were most likely so fatigued that the plane was unable to withstand the updrafts and came apart. Parents and children all had something for which to never cease praising the Lord for His care for us.

I once traveled on a plane in which we had to stand in the aisle because seats had been removed to make room for cargo. We stood in the aisle like we were on an overcrowded bus. The plane was so loaded that we wondered at the wisdom of staying on board. We wondered if the plane could get off the ground. That was one problem. The other was landing the plane without it breaking apart. Of course we made it, or I would not be writing this book.

Once when traveling from Riohacha to Santa Marta with the whole family to attend a conference, the plane ran into rain and cloud cover around Santa Marta. Santa Marta comes right up out of the ocean and rises into the Sierra Nevada Mountains. The airport is on the beach and is approached by coming in off the Caribbean Sea. The plane got lost in the cloud cover. If the pilots made a mistake, the plane could crash into the mountains. I was seated where I could see into the cockpit and what I saw was not very encouraging. The pilots were arguing and looked panicky. They were yelling back and forth to each other and waving their arms and I knew they did not know exactly where they were in relation to the mountains. Suddenly, there was a break in the clouds and we could see the ocean below us. The pilots went down through the small opening before it closed, and off to one side we could see Santa Marta and the airport right beside us. The plane landed and did not continue the flight to Barranquilla.

So much for planes. Traveling by taxi was an experience, too. I once rode in a taxi that had almost no floor boards. Holding my feet to the sides, I could watch the street going by underneath. The floor was rusted out. I jumped into the taxi before looking, never expecting to find no floor, and the driver took off before I had a chance to get out. I was once in a taxi that ran head on into another taxi, and very fortunately at slow speed. The drivers blamed each other and each demanded payment for damages. I checked the taxis and the damage was minimal. Both cars were still in running order and able to take us where we needed to go. After an hour of haggling and arguing, our driver motioned us to get in the car and away we went. He complained bitterly to us about the bad drivers on the Colombian roads. Since we were in the taxi when it collided with the other vehicle, Betty and I

This was the main transportation for a lot of people. Five passengers to a seat, passengers and cargo on the roof, and more people and animals in the truck bed. Before we had our own vehicle this was our means of travel, also.

knew that it was our driver's fault. He, of course, would never admit it.

Not many people in the Guajira peninsula owned their own vehicles like we do in the States, and rarely just for pleasure. They were owned for business purposes. In fact, there were very few cars. Most vehicles were pickup trucks and larger. Pickup trucks were often used for taxis, hauling people back and forth between towns, villages and hamlets. During our first term in Colombia, which lasted three and a half years, we did not own a vehicle and depended on public transportation to get around, mostly buses. Most of the buses in the Guajira were of a homemade variety. The chassis with the engine and cab was purchased, and the cab was removed leaving the windshield. The doors, roof and all were discarded, probably sold somewhere. A wooden framework was built onto the chassis with a solid roof, benches that stretched across the bus, and a truck bed built onto the back. Some had as many as five benches and could seat five to six people per bench. The roof was strong enough to carry cargo and passengers. The truck part also carried animals and cargo. There were carpenter shops that specialized in building these buses. In later years, when the highway was built along the coast, bus companies from Barranquilla that had better buses, sent them up to Maicao, covering all travel points in between. A few of their buses had air conditioning that sometimes worked, otherwise, air conditioning was an open window.

In the 1960's, travel from Maicao to Barranquilla had to be made by driving around the eastern side of the Sierra Nevada Mountains. Much of this was over dirt roads, and it took about twenty four hours to get from one point to the other. That is, if there were no break downs or bridges out. The Colombian government had been working on the construction of a highway along the coast, and after several years of labor, opened it up to traffic. It was a very nice highway that reached all the way to the Venezuelan border. One could then travel from Maicao to Barranquilla in six to eight hours. It was at that time that the major bus companies introduced Greyhound type air conditioned buses with rest rooms, some of which made express trips from Maicao to Barranquilla with just one stop in Santa Marta. Of course, the fare was a mite and a shekel higher, but it was worth it. We often traveled at night because it was cooler and we could get a little sleep, making the trip seem even shorter.

The economy of the peninsula was based majorly on contraband traffic. The goods came in from the Islands of Curacao, Bonaire and Aruba. The launches came in at clandestine ports along the northern tip of the peninsula and goods were moved down to Maicao by large trucks that traveled in caravans. They were taken to large warehouses in Maicao and distributed to merchants who had ordered them, who in turn sold them over the counter in their stores. I never knew the inner workings of the market and always made it my business to remain uninformed about it. We were there to preach the gospel of the grace of God, not to reform the culture and change the customs of the people. When the Colombians were won to Christ, we taught them the Word of God and let the Holy Spirit work in their lives to bring about changes they felt were dishonoring to the Lord.

I owned three vehicles at different times while in Colombia. The first one was a British built Land Rover, four wheel drive. I never used it because it was in bad condition. When I bought it, I thought I was buying a Willys Jeep. When it was delivered to me, it was the Land Rover. The owner had a story, which I never quite understood, about why he couldn't sell me the Jeep. John Bremen, our Missions best mechanic, helped me move the Land Rover from Riohacha to Fonseca where he lived. As he had time and I had funds to pay for parts, he worked on it for months to make it usable. We felt it best to sell it, so we took it back to Riohacha and put a for sale sign on it. We knew it would not be reliable to help us in the work. Three men showed up with the cash and bought it.

We took many rides on the homemade buses during our first term. This was not easy with five small children. Betty did a remarkable job making these trips as easy as she could. There were certain things we always carried

114

with us when we traveled as a family. There was a bag of wet wash cloths, a couple towels, toilet paper, drinking water, bottles of milk as needed, and a snack for the older kiddies. As you might surmise, we did not do a lot of traveling our first term.

At the beginning of our second term, which began in 1965, I began looking for our own vehicle. I found a Willys Jeep in Barranquilla. It was in good condition and gave us several years of good service. I punished it a lot and it forgave me much. We could not have lived out among the Wayuu in Merachon without transportation, and it had to be four wheel drive. I installed a second generator on the engine block which I could use as needed. It put out 110 volts. All I had to do was install a pulley belt, tighten it up, turn the engine over, and we had electricity with a cable to adjust the rpm's. Betty could iron with it. The main purpose was to travel around to various Wayuu rancherias in the evenings and show them slides of Bible stories. We hung up a sheet on the side of their house, plugged in the slide projector and a tape recorder. We had a Wayuu friend translate the stories into the Wayuu language and we had a whole box of these stories with cassette tapes to accompany them. We found that visual aids were a great help in getting across Biblical ideas. When we left Colombia in 1969 for a break from the work, I reluctantly sold the Jeep so we could get money for airfare to the States. Besides, there was no safe place to store it while we were away. I passed the generator on to another couple along with the tapes and slides.

When we returned for a third term in 1971, we bought a Jeep truck. It was new, coming with just a chassis, an engine and a cab. No bed. I bought it in Barranquilla and drove it to Riohacha where I contracted with a carpenter shop to build a bed. He built one exactly like I wanted, made it good and strong, and it served us well for the next eight years. After eight years of hard labor, it was beginning to show the ravishes of time and work. Our service in Colombia was coming to a close, so it was sold, once again providing funds for our move to the States. Soon after buying it, I installed a second oil filter, so the oil was filtered twice. The second filter used a roll of toilet paper and it was amazing how much junk was cleaned out of the oil. As a result, the engine never burned oil, and it was in good working condition when it was sold. The one main problem I had with the truck was that I could not keep the gas tank from leaking. The roads were too rough and bumpy and constantly broke the fitting loose. I bought a hundred pound propane tank, had a welder install a spout with a gas cap, and strapped it into the back of the truck. It never leaked, but it did rust on the inside and I was kept busy keeping the gas filters cleaned out. I installed a second gas filter to help with this problem. I also installed a 24 volt electric switch from an airplane in the gas line. When shut off, the gas would not flow. If anybody

115

attempted to steal the truck, they would not get far with the switch off, perhaps two blocks. The on/off trigger was hidden under the front seat, and the switch under the truck was hidden in the frame of the chassis. It would take someone a while to figure out the system before they could trace the lines and find the trigger under the front seat. I did this because stealing vehicles was big business in the Guajira.

The family vehicle we purchased in 1971. Four wheel drive Jeep truck, a necessity for living in the desert and for hauling family, water, Indians and everything else.

We had a large solid crate in the back of the truck. When we went to Maicao for supplies, everything was placed in the crate which was then padlocked.

The truck was wonderful for hauling water from the windmill. Because I hauled so many heavy loads, I installed extra leaves in the springs, back and front to handle the heavy work.

Over the years the Lord provided for us a way to reach the Wayuu Indian tribe by providing the necessary transportation. He then enabled me to maintain the vehicles, even though I was far from being a mechanic. Only once when traveling with the family did we have a breakdown along the road. A broken main spring on the front of the truck affected the steering. We credit the Lord for keeping us from having accidents, for protecting us from robbers, and for helping us through severe driving conditions. We counted on Him for so much and found the Lord to be wonderfully reliable.

Donkeys were the Wayuu Indians main means of transit. They were also beasts of burden and could carry heavy loads.

CHAPTER ELEVEN

Our Daily Bread

And having food and raiment let us be therewith content.

I Timothy 6:8

People often asked Betty what kind of food we ate in Colombia and how she prepared it. When a person moves to a new country, the culture often makes it necessary to learn new kinds of food. This means new tastes and new ways to prepare food. No matter how good the new food tastes, we often don't like it, perhaps because of the texture, the color, or the way it's prepared. We found that most of the food we ate in Colombia was good food, and if there was something strange about it, we soon acquired a taste and it became part of our daily fare.

During our first term, when we lived in Riohacha, Betty began learning from our neighbors. They taught her how to prepare rice the Colombian way. Every morning I walked a mile to the public market at the edge of town and bought food for the day. Without a refrigerator, we had to buy some food daily, like meat, when it was available. Meat was not sold in cuts like in the States. A carcass was hung on a hook in a stall at the meat market and chunks were cut off. Most of the time, it was required to buy some bones along with the meat. This was fine with us because Betty could make soup, which when left in a pressure cooker could be kept a couple days. Many times I did not know what part of the cow I had bought, and Betty was not sure how to prepare it. We bought a meat grinder and sometimes made hamburger. One time I came home with a chunk of meat that looked strange. We wondered if it was horse or donkey, but it sure didn't look like beef. Though it was different looking it tasted all right.

Always available were eggs, red beets, carrots, cabbage, potatoes, tomatoes and rice. We also had an assortment of fruit like several varieties of bananas, oranges, mangoes, pineapples, and an assortment of tropical fruits. We were told that only men did the marketing, but this turned out to be false information. I saw more women than men at the market. I did the marketing because it had to be done before breakfast and it was too hard to take the whole family and walk a mile to the market and then carry everything back home.

One day when buying some eggs at the market, a man approached me and said eggs were for sale at his house which was just a short distance down the road from the market. Since I was always trying to get acquainted with people and make new friends, I went with him and saw that he had a fair sized flock of chickens. I began buying eggs from him regularly. I paid the same price as was charged at the market, but I knew they were fresher. He liked my business because he could not get that price by selling eggs to the vendors at the market. I was surprised when I went one day to buy eggs and saw his daughter and realized she was a girl that worked at a store in town where I shopped and she had waited on me many times.

At first I did not know the names of foods and bought them by pointing and grunting. I soon learned that pointing with the hand is considered vulgar, so was taught to point with the chin. I compiled a list of names of food and learned the names of some of the vendors. I discovered that the vendors liked to sell to me because I always had the exact change. They also liked to overcharge me because I did not know what the fair price was, and because I did not know how to barter. In fact, I did not have a sufficient command of Spanish to know how to barter and was too timid to do so. I argued that these people were poor and it was not right to argue them down to a lower price. In time, I overcame my shyness. Many people bought food with a promise to pay the next day (*mañana*), a practice that led to a lot of squabbling about money that was owed and how much. Some would insist that they had already paid, though it was doubtful.

There were a lot of stores around Riohacha where we learned to shop for items like coffee, tea, (Lipton's and McCormick's), cheese, chocolate, salt, sugar, oatmeal, (Quaker's) and powdered milk (Borden's). Fresh milk was sometimes available but we never bought it. It was sold in the streets in unclean bottles, often by the Wayuu who had cattle and came into town to sell it. There were bakeries around town, unlike any U.S. bakery. Bread was baked in a back yard kiln and displayed in glass store cases that had flies and roaches crawling around. No doubt the mice and rats also visited at night. We mainly bought two kinds of bread called *pan de sal* (salt bread) and *pan de dulce* (sugar bread). Betty always toasted the bread carefully, not only because of conditions in the glass cases, but because the bread was handled with unwashed hands by the vendors. Any food that was eaten raw or with the rind or peel attached, was first cleaned in water with permanganate to kill germs. Betty took no chances but made sure everything she served was clean.

Riohacha had two hardware stores which I frequented often. When I ceased to point at what I wanted, I found that merchants were willing to work with me, even teaching me the names of things. Getting waited on in most stores was an experience. If a person enters a store and expects to be waited on American style, they may be left standing for a while. The merchants do not often say, "May I help you". Instead, the customer enters the store and loudly announces what he wants. Learning to speak up was difficult for me, especially in the beginning with my poor Spanish. Learning to speak better Spanish and getting over my shyness went together. In time I learned to speak up.

One of the many things Betty learned to prepare was *platano*, which in English is called plantain. It is a cooking banana, only edible if cooked. It can be prepared when it is so green the skin has to be peeled off with a knife. When it is green, Betty would peel off the skin, cut the platano into round slices, fry them, and then squash them on a cutting board with a mallet. Then she would salt them on both sides and fry them a second time. They were so good! When they were yellow ripe, Betty would cut them lengthwise into slices and fry them. They were very sweet and delicious. When the skin on the platano turned black, she would peel off the skin, cook the platano and add to it a natural red food coloring called *hichote*, and serve it with white farmers cheese sprinkled on it. It made a wonderful desert. You cannot imagine how good it was. We all learned to love platano. Betty also cooked it in soup but this was not our favorite way.

Yucca was a staple in our house. It is a tuber, rather long with a brown skin which is removed for eating. It comes in various sizes and is not very nutritious, but it is always available. It made a good filler for a meal and can be fixed different ways. Betty cooked it in soup, fried it and boiled it. Our favorite way was fried, and it went great with a piece of fried meat. Betty would cut it into sticks about three inches long, fried them in a skillet and served them browned.

We usually had some *panela* on hand. Panela is sugar direct from the sugar cane plantations up in the mountains south of us. Sugar cane grows quite tall. When it is cut, it is hauled to a press. Many plantations had their own press called a *trapiche*. As the cane is ran through the press, the juice pours out and runs into a pan which is over a fire. This boils away the water and leaves the sugar. The sugar, which is brown in color, solidifies in the pan and when it reaches a certain thickness of about three inches, it is removed from the fire and immediately cut into blocks about three inches wide and six inches long. It is set aside to dry and harden, and it gets so hard a person could use it for a hammer. Betty cooked with panela using it moderately. Pure, raw cane sugar, unrefined, is good to eat. We did not let our kids eat much of it because it is hard on the teeth. All the public markets and stores carried panela.

Colombia is famous for its coffee. Coffee is served everywhere. In the morning, many families arise to a cup of *café con leche*, (hot coffee with hot milk) and a piece of dry bread to go with it. Breakfast comes later. Later in the day *tinto* is served. Tinto is strong coffee boiled with sugar in it. Without the sugar, tinto is bitter and too strong to be enjoyed. Tinto is served in small expresso cups, and it is usually one of the first things you get when you visit someone's house. The first time I drank tinto was at the Mission's candidate school in West Palm Beach, Florida in 1958. When I saw the little cups, I thought I would drink it down in one swallow. But I was careful enough to taste it first. Ugh! I announced that where ever tinto was not served was the place to send me. I didn't like it at all. Like many other new tastes, I not only learned to like it, I liked it too much, and every morning I drank a large cup and a half at the beginning of the day. I miss my café con leche and tinto these days.

We bought butter in a can. It was a tad expensive so we went easy on the use of it. I don't remember the brand but it came from the Netherlands. The powdered milk also came from the Netherlands and was called *Klim* which is milk spelled backwards. Betty mixed only as much as we could use in a day.

When living in Riohacha, I went to the beach early in the morning when the fishing boats were coming in after a night of fishing. The fish were bought up very quickly and sometimes vendors at the market got first pick and I got none. Our favorite fish was sierra. Sierra is the Spanish word for a saw, and if you could see the teeth in the sierra's mouth, you would know how the fish got its name. They could deliver a very fierce bite so were handled carefully. Sea turtles were also caught and dragged ashore. They were turned on their backs and in this position would suffocate. We ate turtle only once as it was not plentiful. In later years when we lived in Merachon, we went to Manaure for church services with the Wayuu. They were fishermen and went out on the Caribbean in dugout canoes that had a single sail. The Wayuu also caught lobsters. If they caught a lobster that was too small for the market, they gave it to us. They also used to dive for pearls, but after losing two little girls to sharks, they stopped that practice. The girls would dive to a depth of twelve to fifteen feet with a basket to gather oysters which they brought back to the surface and dumped into the canoe. They would catch another lung full of air then go down for another load. When they had gathered a lot of oysters, they would go ashore and crack them open and find an occasional pearl. The Wayuu told me that in earlier years they never had a shark problem, but at the time we were visiting there, the sharks were plentiful. I don't know what the Wayuu did with the oysters.

Oatmeal was another staple in our house. Betty prepared it the usual way. She also toasted it raw and mixed panela with it which we ate with or without milk. In Marachon, Betty baked most of our bread. She was so diligent about this that we always had bread on hand. She would toast it in the morning to go with our oatmeal and it was so good.

One day when I was shopping in Maicao, I noticed a new store had opened, so I went in to see what they were selling. I was surprised to see canned goods from the U.S. They had cartons of candy bars, so I bought a carton. Then I spied Peanut Butter. I don't remember who manufactured it but it was a well known U.S. brand. I bought a jar and it made a big hit at home. However, the candy bars were a disappointment; they had worms in them. When we had occasion to visit our coworkers, we always took a jar of peanut butter for them. It seems it has always been a favorite American food, thanks to George Washington Carver.

There were tubers we used a few times like *malanga, auyama and niami.* They were used mostly in soup. We never really liked the flavor of these tubers and so didn't buy them often. We learned to like passion fruit, and could often get grapefruit, watermelon and cantaloupe; limes were plentiful, along with tropical fruits like nispero, guanavana and guava. White cheese came in five gallon cans and was salty and like rubber. The big blocks of cheese were dumped out of the five gallon cans and sold by the slice. We usually fried ours, but if we could get a cut from deep on the inside of the cheese, we ate it with a desert made from guava fruit. The two went together so well. We bought five pound boxes of American cheese from which Betty would use it to make cheese sandwiches and other things.

We ate a lot of goat meat. Goats are vegetarians and their meat is very good, and so is their milk, which we bought from the Wayuu. Betty would BBQ a side of goat's ribs and that was a special treat. We did not eat mutton or lamb very often because it contained so much fat. We almost never ate pork, and when we did, it was carefully inspected and then cooked very thoroughly. In the towns, pigs roamed freely and cleaned up the garbage thrown in the streets. The Wayuu kept pigs to keep the land clean since they didn't have outhouses, so you can understand why we didn't buy pork.

At times we had our own chickens and turkeys. The turkeys were big eaters and their meat was tough. We got rid of them. We preferred eggs from our chickens rather than those bought in stores or from the Wayuu whose chickens roamed about eating the same things the pigs ate. Sometimes it was noticeable in the smell of the eggs.

Soft drinks were everywhere but we were never big on them. However, when traveling, we never drank the water, but drank soft drinks like Coca Cola and Pepsi. We carried our own drinking water when we could. Colombia had its own national brands of soft drinks which we drank, but I was suspicious that they might not have been made with clean, sterile water. I would buy a case of soft drinks, mixed flavors, and it would last us weeks. We drank them only for special occasions once a week and half a glass at a time.

In Merachon we had cotton tail rabbits just like those in the U.S. We bought them from the Wayuu who shot them with their home made shot guns. It gave us some variety and gave the Wayuu a few pesos in their pockets.

So as it was, we never went hungry; we always had enough to eat. We considered our daily bread as a provision from the Lord. He gave us the seed in the beginning, and the rain that falls on fertile soil, and the sunshine for warmth and light that the seed might grow and produce a harvest. To God be the glory!

CHAPTER TWELVE

Illness, Health, Doctors and Hospitals

Drink no longer water, but use a little wine for thy stomach's sake and thine often infirmities.   *I Timothy 5:23*

Sickness is part of life and is very common. It is more common in places where sanitation is little known and practiced. Some forms of sickness are serious while others are of minor consequence. It is a fact that water is a carrier of disease when it is impure. If it is taken from defiled sources and is untreated, those who drink it are at risk. It behooves the drinker to exercise great care what he consumes.

The Bible verse used above has been said to be the alcoholic's favorite verse. It seems that what is meant by "wine" is that which contains alcohol. Thus, alcoholic drinks may have had medicinal purposes. In Bible times water was probably often polluted and unsafe to drink, but people drank it anyhow. Those who drank contaminated water were naturally infected with disease caused by parasites and other impurities. In many places in the world today, this is still the case, making it necessary to avoid public drinking water. With the array of medicines available today, drinking wine is unnecessary.

On one occasion Betty and I were invited to visit some Wayuu in a remote area north of Uribia. They were new to us and showed an interest in hearing the gospel. When we arrived at their "rancheria", they received us kindly, and true to custom, prepared for us a cup of coffee. We saw that the water they used came from a water hole near their house. We also saw a pig wallowing in the same pool of water, and a cow came for a drink while we were there. The coffee had a familiar barnyard odor to it, but it still tasted like coffee. We did not want to offend our hosts, so we held our breath and drank it, praying and trusting the Lord to protect us from the living parasites that were surely in the water. We survived. The coffee was probably fairly safe because it had been boiled sufficiently to kill any living organisms.

Betty and I served as a nurse and doctor to many Wayuu who came to our house for treatment. I must have given over a thousand injections over the years in Merachon. Many of them were for TB, which is so prevalent among the Wayuu, plus an assortment of other ailments. We bandaged them, gave them pills, cleaned their wounds and washed many cuts and bruises.

The Indians suffered from an unusual ailment we called TBP. It stands for Total Body Pain. They would complain that their head hurt, their arms hurt, their stomach hurt, their legs and feet hurt; everything hurt. They often told us this with a smile on their face. In fact, nothing hurt really; they told us this hoping we would give them a pill that would prevent an illness should one happen to afflict them. It was a preventative measure. We had a bottle that contained five thousand aspirin tablets and this is what they were after. We learned a trick from our good missionary co-workers, Bob and Ruth Ann Moyer. Give them an aspirin tablet and tell them to suck on it. After that, their requests for pills diminished greatly. I once saw the Wayuu take an aspirin tablet, grind it into powder and rub it on a small wound. We didn't know if it did him any good, but he thought it did.

The Wayuu are of a racial stock called Mongoloids. For some reason, Mongoloids do not tolerate measles. An epidemic can wipe out a whole village of Indians very quickly, so it is a serious illness. We treated many Wayuu with measles and lost very few. Most of the Wayuu we knew who died succumbed to tuberculosis. This disease is so common we think most of the Wayuu have it to some degree.

When we first moved out to Merachon, it was not surprising to learn that many of their babies died before they reached two years of age. The lady who lived nearest us had thirteen babies over the years. Four lived to adulthood, and one of them died before reaching thirty years of age from TB.

Wayuu
children

125

The Wayuu were afflicted with a skin disease called maranyas. The maranya began as a pimple, usually on the arms and hands, and grew into a large nasty looking boil. They were painful and left an ugly scar. We had no idea what caused maranyas nor how to treat them. Studies were conducted by several doctors to determine the cause. Doctors concluded from their studies that it was from handling goats, especially milking them. We did not know if this was the real cause or a medical guess.

We treated an assortment of wounds, from gunshots to thorns in the flesh. Our children brought one of their Wayuu playmates to us who had a thorn. I tried to pull it out but without success. I even got hold of it with pliers but it would not budge. Instead, it broke off at the flesh. I never did succeed and it must have grown out in time by itself.

A family of Wayuu, whom we did not know, came by the house one afternoon with a little boy we guessed was about eight years old. He had a badly infected ear. Puss was running down the side of his face; we had never seen such a mess. Betty got a syringe with a bulb and commenced to clean away the puss and mess to see inside the ear. She could see something black and asked for tweezers. She carefully reached in and pulled out a big black insect. We could not tell what it was but it was dead and decaying in the ear. Betty flushed and washed out the ear carefully and it looked so much better when they left the house. We asked them where they lived but they wouldn't tell us; it was their secret. We never saw them again but wondered if the boy's hearing was affected. That, too, will remain a secret.

A young Wayuu, who came by our house many times, showed up one day with a rag wrapped around his hand. He had accidently shot himself with his homemade shotgun. He had been hunting and was walking along the edge of a road when he heard a vehicle coming. He hid his gun under some bushes because he thought it might be Colombian soldiers who would confiscate it. The vehicle passed by without stopping and it was not soldiers. He reached under the bush to retrieve his gun. It was loaded and ready to fire. A twig must have caught on the trigger and it went off, hitting him square in the palm of the hand. We took him into Uribia to the doctor's office. The doctor told me the hand looked like hamburger. He picked out some of the shot, bandaged the hand and that was it. It was all he could do. We don't know what became of the boy because he never came back to our house after that.

We were thankful for the doctor and the hospital in Uribia. The doctor always treated us kindly, even when I took patients to his house. The hospital was not the best. It had a room for surgery which had a broken glass window and a dirty floor. The nurses were nuns and were very kind and helpful. Our youngest son, Michael, was born in that hospital and the nuns delivered him. There was a doctor allocated to Uribia by the government on a temporary basis but he had never delivered a baby and wasn't sure what to do. The nuns knew exactly what to do.

I had an arrangement with the Wayuu in our area. They suffered from many things which required medical attention. I would take them to the doctor or the hospital when they needed help. No charge, of course. However, if medicine was prescribed, I made them pay for it. If they had money for whiskey and other things, then I figured they had enough to pay for something as important as medicine. They usually did. When they pleaded that they had no money, I left that problem for them and the drug store to work out. One thing Betty and I refused to do was help in the delivering of babies. The Wayuu women had too many problems in delivering. If we had been helping a woman deliver a baby and she died, we could have been charged by the Wayuu for her death. Then we would really have had some problems. If they encountered some difficulty, we rushed them to the hospital. They usually went willingly.

On one occasion when I was traveling, I passed through the airport in Riohacha and saw some Wayuu waiting for a plane. One Wayuu man had a towel up to his face. His family told me the man made a homemade pistol and the first time he fired it, the bolt came flying back off the stock and hit him in the eye. He got help from family members, some of whom knew Spanish and they were taking him to the hospital in Santa Marta which had advanced facilities for treating him. He was in great pain and our hearts went out to him in his suffering.

Way too many times the Wayuu waited too long to get help. A family once showed up at our house with a little girl we estimated to be around eight years old. They said she was sick, and it was obvious to us she was very sick. She could barely raise her head. We knew she was serious and offered to take the family to the hospital in Uribia immediately. To our surprise, they told us they had already been there and handed me a bag of medicine prescribed by the doctor. We studied the medicines and had never heard of them before. One was an injection and that was why they came to our house. We prepared the syringe and gave her the shot as quickly as we could. Too late! They lived about four miles away and that precious little girl died on the way home. If they had only taken her to the hospital when she first became sick, we are sure she could have been saved. They didn't want to spend the money on medicine and hoped she would recover on her own. When word came the next day that she had died, we wanted to cry. What a waste!

Bites from animals were uncommon. We treated some pig bites which the Wayuu got when chasing pigs to take them to the market. The pigs had no intention of being caught and would put up a fight and would sometimes inflict painful bites. We always suggested a tetanus shot and they almost always refused. They didn't want to go to the hospital and they didn't want to pay for a shot. They always managed to survive. There were occasional dog bites. Snake bites were rare. We never personally knew a Wayuu who had been bitten by a snake but knew two Colombians and an American who died from snake bites. This is somewhat surprising because we had a large number of venomous snakes. Other bites like those from ants, bees and spiders were common and the Wayuu tended themselves when bitten.

We had lots of scorpions around the house and a scorpion sting is no laughing matter. I was stung so many times I lost count. As best as I can remember, Michael was the only one of our family to get stung and it turned out to be a large scorpion which delivered a nasty infliction. There are many varieties of scorpions around the world, and some are much worse than others. Some have serious poisonous stings while others have a sting like a mild bee sting which feels like an electric shock. Our scorpions were of the mild variety. Scorpions are not all bad. They are good for eating other insects so for this reason we did not always kill them when we found them in the house. Michael did not seem to have any ill effects when he was stung by a scorpion, but such was not the case when he was stung by a bee. We did not know he was allergic to bee stings. A sting on the leg caused his leg to swell from his foot to his hip until it looked like his leg would split open. The swelling went down overnight but we were cautious about bees after that. There was a type of bee that looked especially brutal. It was black and as large as a quarter. It had sharp mandibles with which it bored into wood making a hole big enough to crawl into and make a nest. Since they never bothered us, we didn't bother them. We always wanted to catch at least one and put it into a bottle of formalin so people could see how large these creatures were.

As a family, we stayed amazingly healthy. We suffered very little from illness, infections and disease, and there were no serious emergencies with two exceptions. Already mentioned is the sickness our children suffered from eating castor beans. During our first term of service, which lasted from February 1961 to June 1964, I had two attacks of kidney stones. With the first attack, I had no idea what was wrong with me and went to Barranquilla and spent eighteen days in the hospital under the care of an American doctor, Dr. George Kollmar, at the Baptist Clinic. The stone eventually passed, saving further procedure.

I once fell backwards into a patch of cactus. My truck had a flat tire on the road and I had it on a jack to put on a spare. I heard the truck creaking and knew it was falling off the jack and backed away from the truck. As I backed up, I stumbled over a deep rut in the road and fell backwards into a cactus patch. From this painful experience I learned one thing. If falling backwards into a patch of cactus is bad, having to turn over and crawl out of it is worse. I had so many thorns in me they couldn't be counted. A few stayed embedded for years. Three years later one was extracted from my hand by a doctor in the States. The thorn had penetrated the bone on my finger and was pulled out with some effort.

I also suffered from migraine headaches all the seventeen years we lived in Colombia. These were especially bothersome, usually very painful and made me sick to my stomach. The migraines were on one side of my head or the other but never on both sides at once. When I returned to live in the States, I developed heart problems, and the medicine prescribed by my doctor for my heart also served to prevent migraines. What a blessing it has been to have relief from migraines. The tendency to suffer from migraines seems to have been passed on to some of my children. Betty stayed healthy which was a huge blessing. She worked very hard taking care of her family and we give her the credit for the good health the family enjoyed. Of course, we praise the Lord and give Him credit for His wonderful care for us over the years.

CHAPTER THIRTEEN

The Wayuu Church

And the Lord added to the church daily such as should be saved. Acts 2:47

We often think of a church as a building where people meet for worship. The biblical use of the word refers to the people who meet for worship rather than the building in which they meet. People can be a church without having a building for worship. I have seen videos of people in Russia who walked some distance out of town and about a mile into a forest and stood ankle deep in snow to hold a worship service. The church met secretly among the surrounding trees, and they were, in God's sight, as much a church as people in other countries that meet in buildings with stained glass windows.

When Betty and I went to Colombia in 1961, as far as we know, there was no church among the Wayuu. There was an occasional man or woman who had heard the gospel and believed it, but to their own confession, there was no such thing as an assembly of believers. Our goal was to establish a church among one of South Americas large tribes of indigenous nations. We first planned to preach and teach the Word to the lost so they could know how to be saved. As the Wayuu were saved, we wanted to teach them the Word so they could be stable believers. And then seek out from among them some who could do the teaching to their own people and train them. It isn't because the gospel had never been preached to the Wayuu before we arrived in Colombia, for it had. Mr. and Mrs. William Thompson were among the first missionaries from the South America Indian Mission to witness to the Wayuu. There was one convert, Fransisco Pimienta, whom we have referred to in earlier chapters. He wanted missionaries to come and teach his people the Word of God. I do not know of any other believers among the Wayuu.

I met Fransisco Pimienta before I learned to speak Spanish so our meeting was brief, but we did get acquainted as time went by. I once rode four hours by horseback with Orland Corwin out to Francisco's rancheria to visit him and meet his family. I could not tell if they were excited to see us, but we were well received. The purpose of the trip was to see if it would be possible for Betty and me to move out to where he lived and build a house. Francisco did not think it was a good idea because I did not yet have a command of Spanish, but hoped in the near future I could begin a ministry among his people.

Clarita, age 18, Fransisco's daughter, pictured here with her brother. She was shot and killed by her husband, preventing our move among Fransisco's family.

Though plans were made, the move never happened. Francisco had a daughter who was about eighteen years old when I met the family. She had been promised to a Wayuu man when she was a very young child. She had no say in the matter and as she grew older, made it very clear that she did not want to marry this man. However, the day came when he came to collect his bride and she went off to live with him in another part of the Guajira peninsula. The man was unhappy with his new wife and accused her of immorality. He said he paid for a Miss and got a Mrs. She denied his accusations. He could have returned her to her family which she would have preferred, but instead he killed her. As the story was told to me, she was preparing his breakfast one morning, sitting by the fire on the ground, the usual way the Wayuu cook, and he began to argue with her. He was a known killer and had a gun with several notches in it indicating how many he had killed. His family said he went into their house and came out with a rifle. His family tried to persuade him to not do this deed for it would surely cause a lot of trouble. He shot her right between the eyes and then two more times. The family informed Francisco of her death and he and his brothers went to claim her body. The family got together to discuss what to do. Because the killing was so senseless and because he could have returned the girl to her family, they decided the deed was unforgiveable and declared war on the man's family. Francisco was not in favor of this decision. Being a believer in the Lord, he thought there was a better way. His family thought differently as there were no believers among them. A large number of Wayuu formed a war party, went to the area where the girl was killed, slaughtered several of the family members and burned their houses to the ground, some with the frightened people huddled inside. This incident took place in 1963. It was the beginning of a war between the families that is

131

going on yet today. I met with Fransisco a few days after his daughter was killed and he told me that Betty and I could never move out to or near his family because we would be identified with his family and be in grave danger.

We were broken hearted over everything that happened and felt for all the Wayuu involved. Evidently, God had other plans for us. In 1962 we moved from Riohacha to Uribia and it was during those two years there that I met Guillermo Estrada. He made it possible for us to locate among the Wayuu near Uribia and that is where the Wayuu church began to form. We located in Merachon and from the first days that we were there, we talked to them about the Lord. It seems that a veil was over their eyes and they understood nothing. It takes time and patience to reach the lost.

It was four years before anybody responded to what we were teaching them. We not only had regular services in Merachon, but went to the town of Manaure for services twice a week. Some of the Wayuu youth, who were friends of our children, went with us and joined in the services. These same young people were also in our school where they heard the gospel in every class. They had learned to read and could read the Bible for themselves. One day our children brought two of the girls to Betty and me and told us they wanted to be saved. We sat down with them and explained what being saved meant and how they could become believers in the Lord. They prayed and received Christ as their Savior. This marked the beginning of the Wayuu church in Merachon.

A church service under an enramada on the beach in Manaure. Ruthie is seated in the front.

There were also many Wayuu who came to know the Lord in Manaure and we had good meetings with them twice a week. We did not have a building in which to meet so we met on the beach under an enramada where they lived as most of the men were fishermen. A brisk breeze came in off the ocean and blew sand around as we were singing. I got more than one mouthful of sand as I preached. I had to handle my Bible carefully to keep the wind from tearing its pages. After several years of meeting on the beach and later in the back yard of a house further inland, we helped the Wayuu build a house for services. It was nice to be protected from the constant wind and the torrid desert sun. For many meetings the benches were filled and there was standing room only.

Betty and I standing by the front entrance with a Wayuu family who attended the services.

We also began services on the outskirts of Uribia where some Wayuu lived. Some were well educated and spoke better Spanish than I ever did. We were invited to visit a place called Ichiein, a half hour drive northeast of Uribia. Wayuu were being saved and occasionally would come from Manaure, Uribia and Ichiein to Merachon to join in services there.

While all this was going on, there were Wayuu coming to know the Lord in Maicao under the ministry of Winfield and Frances Buckman. Some of their young men became pastors and are still serving the Lord today, long after the missionaries have departed. They have had an impact on the Wayuu culture which has brought about some changes in how they live and think. These changes are what bothered the Colombian anthropologists and government officials. They said we were changing the culture by changing their customs and they didn't want to see that happen. Their goal was to keep the culture intact. The fact is, Christianity definitely has an impact on a culture that brings about changes.

133

Over the years, the missionaries and the Wayuu worked together spreading the gospel from one corner of the Guajira Peninsula to the other. Today there is a strong growing Wayuu church of Christians. They are being served by several Wayuu pastors. They have their own schools and a Bible and pastor training program. They operate a radio station and broadcast the gospel in their own language. There are no missionaries from the South America Mission living among them at the time of this writing. The Summer Institute of Linguistics has translated the New Testament into the Wayuu language. The SIL workers have also produced music and text books in Wayuuniki and many of the young people have grown up learning Spanish. Was the effort and sacrifice worth it all? Was the money given well spent? Ask the Wayuu! Many who would never have heard the only way under the sun for a lost soul to be saved from a hell that never ends have thanked us many times for bringing them the wonderful Word of God. We, in turn, thank those who opened their wallets, withdrew funds from their church mission accounts and gave, sometimes sacrificially from hard earned money, to the missionary endeavor. For all that has been accomplished, to God be the glory for the great things He hath done.

Prayer time in the front room of our house in Merachon. Note the barred windows, concrete floor, cement block walls and doors on the windows which were open day and night for ventilation.

A church service held in our new school room in Merachon. It was hard to get men to attend. It wasn't "macho" to be interested in God and the Bible. There were some men there but only one young boy in this photo.

Wayuu pastors meeting with John Bremen and me at the radio station that they operated in Uribia. These men broadcasted the gospel in the Wayuu language over the radio. This picture was taken in 2002.

CHAPTER FOURTEEN

Fellow Laborers

Whether any do inquire of Titus, he is my partner and fellow helper concerning you: or our brethren be inquired of, they are the messengers of the churches, and the glory of Christ.   *II Corinthians 8:23*

Lest anyone think that we were the only ones who labored in the work of ministering to the Colombians and Indigenous people in Colombia, I thought it right to mention those of the South America Mission who were our coworkers. We did not work alone. For most of our years in Colombia, we lived by ourselves but there was a cooperative effort among us.

In the early years, namely 1961 to 1963, no work was being done by our Mission among the Wayuu in the desert or the mountain tribes of the Arawak and Kogi Indians. Work commenced among them later in the 1960's. Without the help of other missionaries, the beginning of the Wayuu work would have been greatly delayed, or it may not have been started at all. Even as the Apostle Paul had coworkers to help him in the work, so did we. Paul greatly appreciated his partners who labored with him, and we appreciated the help we received from those who helped us. It is only fair that we give them recognition. They shall be listed but not necessarily in the order in which they came to Colombia. As best as I can remember there were a total of twenty five missionaries who came and went during the years of 1961 to 1978. Maps are included in the book to show the locations of places where each person worked.

One missionary couple was left in Colombia when we arrived and one couple was moved in from Bolivia just before we entered the country. Orland and Margaret Corwin had been in Colombia since the early 1940's, making them seasoned missionaries. The first weeks we were in Colombia we lived with them at the mission house on the outskirts of Riohacha while we looked for our own place to live. Orland was a great help with official paper work. He helped us get registered with the Colombian government which issued us resident cedulas, a very important document. When he met us in Barranquilla as we entered the country, he helped us get our baggage shipped by boat from port of entry in Barranquilla to the town of Riohacha in the Guajira Peninsula. When the baggage arrived in Riohacha, he helped us get it out of customs and delivered to our house. Margaret saw to it that we were sufficiently fed. They served as translators on many occasions while we were learning Spanish, and helped us hire a high school student,

David Correa, to come to our house to help us learn Spanish. Margaret was very good at visiting members of the church and took Betty along many times. Both Orland and Margaret are now with the Lord. Their friendship and help will always be fondly remembered.

John and Janet Breman arrived in Colombia in December, 1960, two months before we arrived. They settled in the town of Fonseca, a farming community located between the Andes and Sierra Nevada mountains. They had served one five year term in Bolivia. When it was discovered that the Mission could get new missionaries into Colombia, the Mission asked the Bremans to transfer to Colombia, which they gladly did. John was especially helpful to me in several ways. He gave me very helpful ideas about learning Spanish. John was a gifted mechanic and graciously helped me with the work and maintenance of our vehicles. When I say graciously, that means he was financially unrewarded. I paid for the parts, he did the work. Janet was always a gracious hostess and a good friend to both of us. We enjoyed the visits which were not often, but always a blessing. Their children and ours were about the same ages so they especially enjoyed the visits. We learned much from the experiences they shared with us. Hardly anything beats experience. John and I once took a survey trip of the Alta Guajira. It was a valuable trip that took several days. Neither we nor our Mission knew exactly what the Alta Guajira was like or who lived there. Betty and I were looking for a place to settle among the Wayuu and the trip settled the matter. More Indians lived around the Uribia and Maicao areas than anywhere else and the Uribia area is where we chose to live. John has gone home to be with the Lord. Janet lives in the Gainesville, Florida area.

Harry and Norma Powell. Both were graduates of Moody Bible Institute and like the Bremans, served one five year term with the Mission in Bolivia. Because of the great need for workers in Colombia, they were also asked to relocate and joined the growing missionary team around 1964. They had four boys who were the same ages as our children, so our families were very close. They first lived in Riohacha, but later moved to Fonseca, while the Bremans moved to Dibulla. Harry was always a close friend, and we shared many ideas of theology. We had amiable discussions at length which we both enjoyed. The Powell's shared with us the experiences they had when working in Bolivia which we found interesting and helpful. Harry has now gone home to be with the Lord. Norma is living near Pittsburgh, Pennsylvania.

Ray and Alma Frazier arrived in Colombia around 1964 and took charge of the work in Carraipia. They were also transfers from Bolivia. It seems like the Bolivian field was training grounds for Colombian missionaries. In their second term in Colombia, they moved to the town of San Juan de Cesar, a farming community where there was a chapel and a small group of faithful Colombian believers. We lived in Carraipia for a few months before the Frazier's left for home assignment, and Ray helped us with our Spanish. Both Ray and Alma are now with the Lord

Bob and Ruth Ann Moyer entered Colombia in 1964 while Betty and I were on home assignment in the States. They lived in Carraipia near the Fraziers. Their goal was to locate among the mountain tribes of the Kogi and Arawak Indians. It was after they left Carraipia that we moved to that town from Fonseca. After some survey trips, they found a place to build a mission station which they named Sarachui. It was at the five thousand feet altitude with only a trail to get there. Either one had to take a horse, mule, or donkey to reach Sarachui, or walk from Atanquez, the nearest town. It was a long hike, uphill most of the way. The location gave both the Kogi and Arawak Indians access to their station. They lived there for several years until endangered by guerrilla activity which forced them to leave. The Moyers have always been close friends and we stay in touch to this day. After leaving Sarachui, the Moyers lived in Santa Marta and had an influential part in the work there among the Colombian believers. They are now retired and living in Pennsylvania.

Winfield and Francis Buckman came to Colombia in 1966 after having worked with the Mission in Brazil for many years. Winfield, known to all of us as "Buck", and Francis were the only other Mission workers to work with the Wayuu tribe. They lived all their years in the town of Maicao where their house soon became a Wayuu center. When the Wayuu came to town, they would stop by the Buckmans house to visit and be refreshed. Buck would often take them home with their purchases in his Land Rover and in this manner became acquainted with a large number of Wayuu and learned where they lived. In the garage of their house they started a school for the Indian children which Francis taught. Out of that school came several of the Wayuu pastors who are active in the ministry today, faithfully serving their own people. The Buckmans were indefatigable workers. Their house was also our stopping place when we went to Maicao shopping. We shared a mailbox so once a week we picked up mail at their house. The mail was of the highest priority when our children were in school in Venezuela, as letters went back and forth on a weekly basis. It was a two and a half hour trip from Merachon to Maicao, one way, when the roads were especially good, so we saw each other only when Betty and I went shopping. Time and labor took its toll and the Buckmans retired and moved to Lakeland, Florida. Retirement years were short as both Frances and Buck passed away and are now with the Lord in heaven. Workers trained by both the Myers and Buckmans are now working together serving their own people.

Joe and Molly Messer arrived in Colombia during our third term of service, 1970-1975. They lived in Valledupar and operated a bookstore selling Christian literature and school supplies. The Messers, Myers, Powells, Moyers, and Lees all had children in the school in Rubio, Venezuela and we usually traveled to the school together as a group. The trips were long, a day and a half by bus, (U.S. school bus type), longer for us and Moyers who were farthest away, but the companionship made the travel more bearable. After resigning from the Mission, the Messers located to South Carolina and Molly went back to nursing while Joe became a bus driver for a charter bus company. Joe passed away in 2013 and Molly has retired from nursing and still lives in Lyman, South Carolina.

Steve and Carol Lee arrived in Colombia so Steve could help with electronic things such as the fifty cassette players the Mission had for the work. Steve kept them repaired and even changed the heads on them so that the only tapes they could play were the ones supplied by the missionaries. We wanted those who borrowed the cassette players to hear Bible teaching rather than canteen music. The Wayuu would borrow the players and use them for anything other than Bible lessons. The Lees had three children when they arrived in Colombia so Carol was busy taking care of her family and the household chores. They now live in the States in South Carolina. They have been associated for several years in a jail ministry in Ecuador, helping an Ecuadorian pastor minister to prison inmates.

George and Mary Baker worked in Peru and took a leave of absence for a few years from the Mission. During the time they lived in the States, they were involved in work among Native Americans. Later they came to Colombia and lived in Santa Marta where they had a ministry. George and Mary came to Merachon on one occasion when the young men from Ichiein were visiting us and gave us some good ideas about teaching these men how to teach their own people. When they returned to the States, they began a ministry working with incarcerated people, especially those who spoke Spanish. They did it all by mail and though George and Mary are now both with the Lord, the ministry is still going on and is called Bible Studies by Mail.

Bob and Helen Crump were missionaries in Brazil for many years, working with the Xavante Indians. They were transferred to Colombia so that Bob could assume the duties of Colombian field director for our Mission. He held this position until they returned to the States in 1978. The Crumps have lived in Florida and Tennessee. Bob went home to be with the Lord recently and Helen is now living in Florida.

Jack and Bea Hough came to Colombia in the 1970's and lived in Barranquilla where they established a Christian book store in a strategic location in the downtown area; in fact, across the street from the Cathedral. They lived and worked in Peru for many years where Jack served as the field director the last years they lived there. In Barranquilla they lived in a high rise apartment building. Eventually they turned the bookstore over to a Colombian Christian. The Mission asked them to move to Canada where they served as representatives of SAM for a few years. Jack was severely diabetic which eventually claimed his life. Bea is now living in Florida.

Bert and Marjorie Watson were asked to leave their work in Peru and move to Colombia where he would serve as field director for the Colombian field. They came before Crumps and stayed for two years before returning to Peru to resume their work there. Bert passed away in Peru from cancer. Marjorie moved back to the States and lived in Tampa, Florida until she, too, went home to be with the Lord.

Mary Frazier is the daughter of Ray and Alma Frazier and worked in both Peru and Colombia. She lived in Sarachui with the Moyers for a season and was a registered nurse like Ruth Ann.

Ruth Huber also worked in Peru and transferred to Colombia where she teamed up with Mary Frazier. They lived in Valledupar for a season, and then Ruth moved to Sincelejo. Both are now retired and Mary lives with her husband in New Mexico, and Ruth lives in Lancaster, Pennsylvania.

Connie James arrived in Colombia in the late 1960's and lived in Sarachui, Fonseca, Merachon and Carraipia. She left the Mission in the early 1970's and her whereabouts today are unknown.

This very brief resume leaves out nearly everything interesting about those mentioned above. Each is mentioned with many fond memories of enough experiences to fill a very large volume. There is not enough room to tell of their Christian lives and how it was a blessing to know and work with them. There were no loafers among them. Not one of them came to Colombia for a six month vacation twice a year. They came, rolled up their sleeves, dug in their heels and went to work. Their fortitude produced results that stand today as a monument to their sacrifice, skills and labor. As the years roll by they are slowly going to their reward where each one will surely hear, "Well done, my good and faithful servant."

It seems appropriate to mention two groups apart from the South America Mission who have contributed to the work among the Wayuu, Kogi and Arawak tribes. First, there is the Summer Institute of Linguistics who reduced the unwritten Wayuu language to writing and translated the New Testament into the Wayuu language. This was a monumental task that took years of labor to accomplish amidst numerous difficulties. Rich and Karen Mansen labored for approximately forty years in this project, and were later assisted by David and Linda Captain. The Wayuu New Testament stands as a memorial to their persistent efforts. Karen Mansen, who is now with the Lord, also wrote several songs and choruses in the Wayuu language.

Another group that provided some added help was Gospel Recordings. They came and recorded stories and messages in the Indian languages and produced 78 rpm records of their recordings. They also provided hand cranked record players for the records and later had some equipment for playing CD's. When we could not speak the Wayuu language, the records provided a means for the people to hear the gospel.

Various Wayuu who lived within walking distance of our house. The lady at the top left has her face blackened with a powder that comes from a fungus plant. In the photo next to her, the girl has red markings on her face that comes from a ground-up red stone.

CHAPTER FIFTEEN

A Brief History of the South America Mission

The South America Mission grew out of the work of Dr. and Mrs. Joseph A. Davis who felt led to work as missionaries among the tribal Indians of South America. Dr. Davis organized the Paraguayan Mission in 1914 and opened the first station in the northern part of Paraguay. There was already a group of missionaries from Scotland called the Inland – South America Missionary Union who had been working in that area since 1902. In 1919 the two Missions merged and adopted the name Inland South America Missionary Union which was incorporated in New York in 1921. The goal was to establish self supporting, self propagating churches among the indigenous Indian tribes in South America.

Ill health made it necessary for Dr. and Mrs. Davis to return to the United States. They settled in New York where Dr. Davis served as pastor of a Baptist church in Long Island, New York, a position he held from 1923 to 1928.

In 1932 the two Missions decided to divide into separate Missions. The Mission headed by Dr. Davis retained the name Inland South America Missionary Union until 1940 when the name was changed to South America Indian Mission. In 1970 the name was shortened to South America Mission because the work had expanded to include nationals in urban cities as well as Indians.

Over the years the Mission has reached over thirty Indian tribes and people who were a mixture of Indian and National people of the country. Most of these people lived in remote river areas of the Amazon Valley in the center of South America. Regional headquarters were established in Brazil, Bolivia, Peru and Colombia.

In its endeavor to reach the various tribes and educate them in the Gospel of salvation, the Mission established schools, Bible Institutes, medical clinics, camps and bookstores. Airplane service, called SAMAIR was also added to help reach mission stations in remote areas. The Mission published informative literature like Our Flag and Field, South America Indians, Inland South America and The Amazon Valley Indian. Several missionaries wrote books of their particular work, many still available today. Missionaries did translation work in the unwritten indigenous languages.

The first headquarters in the United States was in Long Island, New York, but in 1931 it was moved to West Palm Beach, Florida to accommodate the deteriorating health of Dr. and Mrs. Davis. At a later date, the Mission moved to South Carolina about twenty five miles southwest of Charlotte. In 1982, a Canadian branch was established in Guelph, Ontario.

From the time of its founding to the publishing of this book, over three hundred missionaries have served the Lord under the South America Mission. Having personally known many of the missionaries, I can testify that they were diligent, godly, self sacrificing, hard workers who loved the Lord, loved His Word, loved the truth, loved the church and loved the lost. It is certain that every one of them would say TO GOD BE THE GLORY for all that has been accomplished and counted it the greatest privilege to be a part of reaching the lost.

CHAPTER SIXTEEN

Letters Home

My wife, Betty, went home to be with our Lord in November of 2008. Since she is not able to contribute to the writing of this book, I am including the following letters written by her. These letters were written by Betty between 1961 and 1963 to her family while in Colombia. They were mainly written to her father, brother and sister (her mother passed away before we left for Colombia). We share them with our readers as they offer a little glimpse into the life of a missionary worker, wife and mother on the mission field.

Betty and me with three of our children, Ruthie, Jeanette and John Paul. This was taken in 1960, a couple months before we left for our first missionary term to Colombia.

This photo was taken in 1965 in Riohacha, just after we returned from our first furlough. Betty was washing clothes while the children played. The child in diapers is Michael, Jeanette is standing in the background and John Paul is barely visible but is sitting in the hammock.

February 23, 1961

Dear Daddy, Jim, Edith,

Well, I guess you wonder what all we're doing. A week ago yesterday we flew down here to Colombia, that was the 15th. It took about 4 and ½ hours. It was a very smooth trip and we got along pretty well. When we arrived we were the last to go through customs. It was very hot and the children were a handful but we finally made it. No one was there to meet us so we took a taxi to the Hotel Genova. They didn't know what we wanted, but finally someone came along who spoke English. They thought we should go to another hotel but we said no, we're to meet someone here, so we got a room. We struggled through about 24 hours of "no speaka de Spanish" and then at noon on Thursday Mr. Corwin came. He and Whitey ran around while I took care of the children, it was rather hectic. They got our footlocker out of customs which didn't cost us anything. They also bought a bed and chairs for the living room. The chairs are aluminum lawn chairs, 2 rock. They are green and white and yellow and white. Most people down here have lawn or patio furniture.

The houses are mostly cement floors and walls, sometimes brick. Some are painted very nicely. There is running water which has to be boiled.

There is electricity if the plant is running and it hasn't been since we've been here. There are a few toilets which constantly back up because of full cesspools. Otherwise, the street is just about as handy. So all effort must be made to keep clean and wash hands, etc frequently. One outstanding feature of Colombia is the wind which blows the livelong day. And with it comes sand by the bushels. When you hang clothes out to dry they turn the color of sand. The Guajira is semi-desert as it rarely rains. The wind dies down at night but not always.

Anyway, on Saturday we flew up to Riohacha, it took about an hour and 1/3. It was a little bumpy but not bad. I am more or less over being afraid of flying.

We had a bumpy ride to the Corwin home. It is a little outside of town and really gets the dust. It's the kind of place you might camp in at home, but it's what people live in down here. In other words, I have to get used to living here. We all do, if others can do it, so can we but only with the Lords help.

The Corwins are wonderful people. Margaret reminds me of Mom. She has a strong southern accent. They have two children here. Two in the States, a girl and a boy each.

Our Spanish lessons have started. Right now it would be good to hear some English babble. You don't know what it's like trying to understand a bunch of sounds.

I could go and on but time does not permit.

We are well. Ruth and John Paul were a little sick but are over it for now. Write.

Love to all
Betty, Whitey
Greetings to all at church.

March 16, 1961

Dear Daddy, Jim and Edith,

We are finally in our own place. Our baggage arrived on the tenth and we moved that day.

So far we all seem to be pretty well except that we have so much to do we don't get enough rest. It takes about twice as long to cook, clean, and wash clothes as it does at home. We are going to try and get a washing machine. It will save me many hours and much energy. Clothes get twice as dirty twice as fast down here. Another big job is trying to keep the children from contamination and that is a job when water is contaminated and all the dirt is contaminated and much of the food. We boil water, cook all vegetables well, wash fruit with a germicide, etc. One problem is bats in the house. They nest between the ceiling and the roof. It isn't the flying that bothers us so much as their filthy droppings. Rats, of course, are taken for granted.

We have electricity from about noon until six a.m. That is if the plant doesn't break down. The last time we were a week without it.

Life is very different here. Some people have it fairly nice while on the other hand some people have geese wondering in and out of their houses.

We are one of the main attractions in town. Everywhere we go people gawk and stare and exclaim. What a feeling! They think Jeanette and Ruthie are beautiful. Because of the blonde hair they are called "mono".

There are not too many believers but most of them are men and of the better class. It's better to begin that way. A chapel is yet to be built but it will probably be built soon. I play for services on a terribly out of tune piano that makes me wince. We have sung a couple of times in English. Anywhere from two to twenty attend services. They are on Sunday at nine thirty AM, and four thirty PM. and Saturday at seven thirty PM.

Here it is the custom to keep the door open to show yourself hospitable but we have to get a gate first. We open it only when we're expecting our teacher. It is just not done to knock on a closed door.

We have a neighbor who is somewhat of a pest. Today was the first day she didn't prance in. Yesterday she took the liberty of telling me that I shouldn't keep my butter in its original can, so she piled it on a dish and took off with what was left. It's nice to know there isn't too many like her.

I guess we're getting used to living in a barn but we have to try and pretty it up so people won't look down their noses at our "ugly house". I wish I had a least a dozen pair of plastic drapes. Would I be in my glory!

I told Louise to send me one pair air mail. Packages weighing less than a pound sent by air mail first class, generally get through. I surely do hope it works. Plastic drapes are not to be found and material is expensive.

We live on a diet of stringy roasts, potatoes, rice, carrots, papaya, bananas, bread. Other vegetables are not found except such things as dried beans, dried black-eyed peas. We treated ourselves to a two pound box of Kraft cheese at a dollar a pound. There are some American canned goods available but they are high. We were buying local milk but it got to be a bother so now we are using U.S.A. made Klim by Bordens. It's powdered whole milk. Pray that we'll adjust well and that the language will be conquered. It's so hard to find time to study.

P.S. Thank you, Jim for the support.

Love to all,
Betty and Whitey

April 7, 1961

Dear Daddy, Jim and Edith
    How are you all doing? We're faring pretty well, except we're always tired.
    Whitey was off to a conference for a week over Easter. It was pretty lonely.
    An eleven year old girl came to live with us and help us. I'm not sure I like the idea too well. Since I'm not used to having help I don't like to tell her to do things. I'm supposed to have her mop and sweep the floor, do dishes, help with the children, help wash, etc. I'm not accustomed to having eleven year olds do all that. She is tiny for eleven. The people here are mostly all of a smaller build than in the States.

Another thing that bothers me is the fact that Jeanette and Ruthie resent her care of them.

I think we're getting more or less adjusted. It has been over a week since I was homesick. And when I get homesick, do I get homesick! It's awful to feel that way when you know you'll be seeing very little of home for the rest of your life.

Jim, I hope your birthday was happy. I'm afraid there aren't many greeting cards down here.

Communism is striving hard for a foothold here. (In fact, it does have a good foothold.) There is a fellow across the street who says he's not a communist but he likes Russia better than the U.S.A., of course, he has seen neither but the news is Communist screened here and a big issue is made out of the racial problems in the States. It hurts a lot to hear someone talk like that, especially when they don't even know the truth.

Appreciate the United State for its beauty.

There is a girl across the street who told me she is confused because the priest says one thing and the Bible another. Pray that she'll go with us sometime. There are many men believers because the meetings are too far out- beyond the street lights and women just don't walk out that far.

Our washing machine hasn't turned up yet. In case I didn't tell you, a lady in another town was going to buy one for us in Venezuela. I hope it comes soon as I am almost desperate. We finally got an iron which the Lord surely provided. It is a brand new G.E. iron almost exactly like mine in the States. Of course it's rather disgusting since I could have brought mine, oh well. It cost only around ten dollars which is very good. We also have to get an oven and a baby bed. John Paul sleeps with Ruthie. He keeps falling out of bed and they wake each other up. We now have a high chair and a play pen. He likes his high chair but isn't too fond of the play pen.

Jeanette and Ruth like to run over to the neighbors. Sometimes the lady takes them but if she doesn't, do they holler. We have a gate to keep the kids in. If you don't keep your door open at least part of the time then you are unsociable as visitors will always turn away from a closed door.

Our Spanish is coming slowly because of lack of time.

Hope this finds you all very well.

> Lots of Love to all,
> Betty and Whitey
> Jeanette, John Paul, Ruth

April 25, 1961

Dear Daddy, Jim and Edith

Well, we still haven't heard from you but I'd better write again. Do you send your letters air mail? Thanks for John Paul's birthday card.

Jeanette, Ruthie, and John Paul have been sick with diarrhea and vomiting. We think it's amoebic dysentery and are giving them medicine for it. Please pray for them because a good dose of amoebas can take them.

We are getting used to things by now, except for the flies, they are fierce. Ants are also plentiful. At mealtime we sit and eat with one hand while we swing the other around in the air. Don't we have fun?

Our washing machine hasn't arrived yet but we're still hoping. Today I had five sheets and blankets to wash, plus almost all the diapers and other assorted pieces. I told you we have fun.

There are a number of things we have to get yet including a bed for John Paul, and an oven. Whitey wants to make some cupboards, a sandbox, and perhaps tricycles for the kids as they are in desperate need of things to do.

Today the Corwins got permission to build the chapel. Tomorrow they are going to start the ball rolling. It will be done in about two months.

Language study is coming slowly but surely. Pray that we'll be able to learn it well and as quickly as possible. The children still don't understand any of it yet. I believe they're too young to learn it quickly. They've barely learned English. When they do lean, they'll speak it like the Colombians but we'll still have an English accent.

The people here watch all the revolutions with great interest. Communist propaganda runs high and they are working hard among the students. One of the fellows is terribly mixed up about it all and even burned his Bible because of it. He is in a mess and really needs help. I wish Whitey could speak with him.

Whitey's birthday is soon but I guess I won't be baking a cake without an oven. I've asked some others to do this. Could you send some postcards? Enclose one with each letter. Pictures that are actual photographs like the Blue Water Bridge and things like that. Also send pictures of yourselves. We wish like everything that we had brought our photo albums.

Love to all,
Betty, Whitey
Jeanette, Ruthie, John Paul

May 28. 1961

Dear Daddy, Jim, and Edith,

How are you all? Taking care of your selves, I hope. We are all doing well except this has been a terribly hot week. A real scorcher. It took away all of Whitey's energy. The children all had a bad heat rash.

We have been listening to two blaring radios with that terrible Colombian music. It's beginning to get unbearable. How they can stand it in the same room I'll never know.

Spanish is coming along slowly. Sometimes it's such a chore. The verbs are killer-dillers to learn. Jeanette and Ruthie say a word or two. "Gracias" (thank you) "Venga" (come), "adios", "hasta luego" (until later).

We caught 19 rats in two weeks with our traps and they are still coming thick and fast.

We got an Altoona Mirror Friday. We asked Louise to order it for every Monday. We received the May 1st edition. We were glad to get it.

I tried giving John Paul a haircut and it sure is ragged. We need clippers. He sure is a doll though. He likes to push his playpen around.

No washing machine yet. I'm hoping for an oven next week.

The cupboards that Whitey made look nice and are a joy to use. He's going to make a wardrobe now.

Mr. Corwin has been working hard on the chapel and goes to sleep every time he sits down. He's about 55 years old.

Soon it's Jeanette's birthday. Do you feel like you have a granddaughter four years old? Louise sent some hair barrettes and 2 small coloring books by air mail. She ought to love the barrettes because she always fusses with her hair. She has three bobby pins she sticks in.

We have been troubled with thousands and thousands of ants. The mud walls are swarming with them.

Whitey is keeping a notebook of the letters we receive and send.

I hear that things are not looking up in the States, especially in the South. It makes you wonder what all, if anything, will come to pass before the Lord comes. Margaret Corwin feels that mission work here in Colombia may have its days numbered because of Communism. It doesn't seem quite that strong yet however.

Bye now, hoping to hear from you soon.

Love to all,
Betty and Whitey
Jeanette, Ruth and John Paul

June 11, 1961

Dear Daddy, Jim and Edith,

I was so glad to finally hear from you. The last letter I got from you was dated May 12. That's quite a long spell.

We're still well and since you are working so hard, you must be all right, too. The house will look nice when you're done. I hope you all can keep it clean enough to enhance its appearance.

It has been hot here all the time, so far. It is cooler in the evening, but it's still hot for sleeping. Maybe that's because of the nets. Although they are sheer, they keep out a lot of breeze. I told Whitey that it will seem funny, when we're at home, not to have to sleep under nets, and also to be able to drink water right out of a faucet. I shall probably always be looking for roaches too.

We don't know what the actual temperature averages. All we know is it's hot! It is dry. There is supposed to be a rainy season but we haven't seen it here in Riohacha. There are 2 towns in 2 different directions about 40 miles away (that's a guess) that get more rain than we do.

There are no gardens or farms here. Practically all produce is brought from Fonseca, one of the 2 towns. Fruit like tomatoes, oranges, papaya, tangerines, bananas, pineapple, are always picked green to bring here because the bumpy rides are too hard on ripe fruit. Consequently they don't usually taste as well as they might when they are tree ripened.

While you are sending pictures be sure to include some of your faces also.

Whitey has partly finished the wardrobe and we are hanging clothes in it. What a relief that is!

Thank you for the two dollars. We shall probably save them as there is nothing she needs at this time and there are no worthwhile toys available. Perhaps sometime when Whitey goes to Barranquilla he'll be able to get something as they have many more things there. It is better if the dollars are exchanged for pesos at the bank. Jeanette had a pretty good birthday. I got a half set of used play dishes from Ruth Corwin and bought her a pair of American socks in exchange. I made a cake and baked it at Corwins. It turned out very well. I made 7 minute frosting. We couldn't get candles though. I am supposed to get an oven the 15th, but that remains to be seen.

Whitey and Mr. Corwin were gone over night to see about the washing machine, but they didn't learn a thing because the lady was in Maracaibo.

Jeanette is getting big and growing out of her clothes. I'm afraid they won't be such little tykes when you see them next. We wish we had brought more toys for them.

In July out of country air mail will cost 15 cents for one half ounce. Until now it has been ten cents. I'm going to try and do something different. I am going to mark each letter in the corner with a letter, starting with "A". If you would mark the letter on a calendar or something, you can tell whether or not you missed one. We are keeping records of all letters received and sent so we will be able to keep track easily. You could do the same thing in return. So if you get an "A" and a "C" you know "B" got lost. Do you suppose you could find more postcards to send?

We are still creeping along with Spanish. There is so little time. However, little by little we understand more. Sometimes I think what fun it would be to understand everything when these people don't realize it. I understand in part but not enough.

Keep well now. Always glad to hear from you. Lots of love to all,

Betty, Whitey, Jeanette, Ruthie, John Paul

July 17, 1961

Dear Daddy, Jim and Edith,

Well, by this time you should have my last letter, I hope. I'm glad the Morris' are doing so well. How is Elsie? She has an awful big adjustment to make with two little ones, I feel like I know very little of what's happening in Port Huron.

Friday we had a real downpour. The clouds really burst their seams for the first time since we've been here. The streets were rivers (no sewers). Half our patio went down the drain. The leaks in our roof dripped like mad. None over our beds, though, isn't that terrific? I had to make mad dashes to the kitchen 'cause it's across the patio. It wasn't so nice while it was raining but for two days after it was so clean and fresh and very little or no dust flew around. It was swell! We're back to normal now.

Wednesday, Lord willing, Margaret and I are going to take Alicia back to Atanquez. We'll have to get up about four. It's a long bus ride from here to there and it may take us two days, depending on connections. We can only get a bus to a certain town and then we have to hail a taxi or a truck for a tortuous up-mountain ride. It takes four hours to go twenty miles. Atanquez is in the mountains where it is very cool at night and rains quite often. Corwins were there 14 years and established a completely indigenous church. In fact, almost the whole village are believers. It is isolated. Few people care to take their wares up there. No radio, no newspaper — they know very little about the world and I guess most of them we would consider country bumpkins. I guess they are a very different people.

We had a prolonged interruption. David, our teacher, came. He was at loose ends. The poor fellow! He's a good guy - intelligent, clean, good-looking. He has nothing to do. He never sees the other Christian fellows, they are all so different from him. Girls ask him to dance, smoke, go to parties, go to shows, and he says no! no! no! and they say idiot, dunce, you're wasting your youth. He has great promises of being able to serve the Lord. It will be sad if he goes astray and wastes it. Pray for him.

Love to all from all,

Betty and Whitey, Jeanette, Ruthie, John Paul

July 28, 1961

Dear Daddy, Jim and Edith,

We have the washing machine. It arrived a week ago. It is brand new and we owe about $500 pesos yet, about $63. Since the lady lives so far it is a matter of getting it there, not the money. It is a pink and white Kenmore. I did two big washings so far since I've been home. When I think what it would be like without, boy am I grateful. While the washing machine was washing merrily away I was getting loads of other things done and I certainly am not nearly as tired. Having this machine here compares almost as well with sending your laundry out in the States. It's wonderful. We're having a terrible time with rats and ants. It will be so good to be located and get into our own house that we can fix up to keep things out.

Next week, we will be going to Fonseca to spend a week with the Bremans. They are a young couple with 3 boys who spent their first term in Bolivia. They wouldn't go back without a plane. The missions said no so they asked to be sent to Colombia. They are living on mission property and are fixing themselves up good. He's building all sorts of things as he is good at things like that. She has a lovely kerosene stove by Perfeccion that makes mine look sick and me look green. My stove is a mess and a good one just can't be bought in Riohacha, kerosene, that is. When Margaret and I were there for supper this week we had tenderloin steak, French fries, tomatoes, melon. It was good! Steak, yummy.

Margaret and I went to Atanquez a week ago Thursday. We took Alicia back too. I might say here that I am so relieved that she is gone. I feel so much better. It was a rough ride and I got pretty sick although I never threw up. We rode on the back of a truck from Valledupar (the jumping off point for Atanquez) to Atanquez. We had a flat about halfway up but it didn't delay us much. The road was rocky and curvy and

153

I was sore from bouncing up and down on the plank (bench). The air got colder as we went higher and cured me of my sick stomach. We finally arrived and oh, I loved it. It's beautiful. Those rugged green mountains! I've never seen anything like them. That place is so beautiful, so peaceful, and so far away from it all. You'd never think about H-bombs up there. You could forget it all. The people live simply but they don't have clocks so they are not worrying about rushing to get things done. The way they know to come to service is by playing the organ for about a half hour. There are many believers there so it really helps the atmosphere. If Jim went there he'd take off in a minute up those slopes. A lot of the men have farms on top of the mountains. They take off for days at a time. They grow cotton, beans, coffee, mangos, pineapple, platano, yucca, avocado, bananas, and livestock. Pigs wander around the rocky and often steep streets like dogs do here in Riohacha. Horses, burros, goats, cows wander over the mountain sides. I like Colombia much better for having been there and my homesickness is gone again.

Bye now. Lots and lots of love from all

October 3, 1961

Dear Daddy and Jim,

Another hot, hot day with almost no breeze. That sun is terrible and it bothers me to go out in it for five seconds. I could use a big straw hat but they don't make them for women here. I don't think Christmas is a very good time to fly. It's always crowded and there seem to be more accidents in winter. It also sounds too expensive.

We have the crabbiest kids in town. I don't know if they are getting sick or just feel house bound. They don't get out much and there isn't much place to play. We need a place with a big yard and lots of shade.

Did I ask you to send the film to Louise? You can tell them to send it back when they're done.

In case you didn't know, the place where it says "first fold" and "second fold" are for writing, too.

News is rather sparse here. I wrote some of it in Jim's letter and I don't see any point in repeating myself.

Whitey is still weak but we're all right otherwise. I'm as lazy as all "git-out" these days.

I've got to be seeing to dinner so I'll close for this time. Take care.

Love, Betty

October 8, 1961

Dear Daddy and Jim,

   Missed a letter from you this week. Hope everything is all right. We're back to normal, I guess. My pen is a wreck from John Paul. It always worked so good.

   Our general director didn't make it this week. He's to come next week.

   Our politician neighbor had a fiesta last night and is continuing it today. There's a bunch of men drinking in front of his house and are they noisy. I'm afraid of drinking men and they don't get many hellos from me, neighbors or not.

   Say, have you been able to do anything about my driver's license yet? I should keep it up.

   If we ever get transportation, all I'd have to do to get a license here would be to show one from the States. Also it will be useful when we return on furlough.

   We've been speculating on what we'll eventually be doing. Right now I'm sort of thinking we'll end up in Corwin's house and they'll be living in town at the chapel. If that's the case I'm hoping we'll be able to get a jeep so we won't have to haul four children through the hot sun to service all the time. We're hoping to find out about some of this when Mr. Norwood comes next month.

   Whitey saw a lovely Frigidaire this week that may or may not be for sale. It's less than two years old and is one of those models with shelves on the door. We're getting so anxious to have a refrigerator and I'm dying to make ice cream.

   One morning this week Margaret Corwin and I went on a wild goose chase for a medical truck that was said to have an American doctor. Someone has told us since then that he is to come in November. Margaret wanted to try and get an examination for me, if possible, to make everything absolutely positive. I would like to have a checkup but we aren't real sold on the doctors here.

   It was the first time since February that I climbed a flight of stairs and I am really out of practice. My heart skipped a beat and my legs felt weak. I'm going to have to break in slowly at home.

   Well, must close. Hope to hear from you soon.
   Love, Betty

February 11, 1962

Dear Daddy,

I have news this week. Our propane gas stove arrived yesterday and what a change it has made. It's a pretty white enamel thing like those at home. Maybe it's not quite as sturdy but it will do. It makes such a difference! It seems to take the work out of meals I don't know how I ever cooked on that other thing. Everything was always so smoky and black it was hardly worth the effort to clean the pots. It's impossible to say what this stove means. It's wonderful to have four good burners. I could only cook on one on the other, it was getting in such awful shape. I used it for 11 months and I think we got our $15 worth out of it. This new stove has helped cheer me up some. Whitey is on the go so much these days or he's always at his desk studying and that only leaves me the kids to talk to and I've been feeling down in the dumps. I hardly go out. There's no place to go when I do.

Our cold weather probably only gets down to the sixties. I hope yours is better by now. It sure sounds rough. I don't think things are too bad in Pennsylvania this year.

It is carnaval time these last few weeks before Lent and people have parties, etc. Last night the people behind us had an orchestra in and it was pretty much an all night affair. I slept through it.

Jim writes to me quite regularly. He outdoes you by a long shot. He even outdoes me he's so prompt.

Tuesday Whitey is going to meet John Breman in Maicao and a group of them will go over to Uribia and sell Bibles and things. Whitey likes to be on the go but it's not so hot being left. Measles are all over but we now have colds.

There seems to be colds going around with a lot of coughing as one of the symptoms.

Well, I hope you are well and coming out on top of things, especially the snow right now.

Love from us all, Betty

P.S. We've been here a year now. It's the fourteenth and I still haven't got this mailed. Whitey's gone and will be back today or tomorrow. Bye

March 10. 1962

Dear Daddy,

I hope the weather is improving. I'm wishing that if you make a change, you'll get to where you can navigate more easily. Being alone out there in such weather makes you feel too isolated. If things get too much, do what you can to get out. We may all be far away, but you're not forgotten and we will be seeing you when possible. Take care of yourself in the meantime. We'll have to live there because we depend on so many people there. The letters are about two weeks apart from me now. Seems like one week goes fast and I can't think of much news.

The mission is on the verge of losing a plot of ground. It is an unused piece across from Corwius and was in the name of former missionaries. In spite of the fact that taxes have always been paid, the land was resold on the excuse that the owners had left. Well, the case is pending but the office that sold it is very bullheaded. Corwins were trying to sell the land when this came up. A representative told one of the believers that the mission shouldn't let the land be taken or they'll try it again. All the property here is in the name of former missionaries. However, prospects don't look bright.

The weather changed here from wind and sand to no wind, a lot of humidity, and some rain. It poured the other night and about flooded the place. Most everything is set up off the floor though so everything was all right. Our beds were okay. Our roof is like a sieve.

A teacher from high school was out last Sunday to service. He is very close to being a believer. He talked like he had been thinking a lot about the gospel.

Last weekend was carnaval - the big bang before Lent. It looked to us like a combination of halloween and New Year's. I guess it comes from the same source as Mardi Gras. Last Sunday morning quite a number of men muddied themselves up from head to toe and went around grabbing people and throwing mud. We stayed home from services. Those men had the street pretty much to themselves. There is a social club behind us and they had a dance about every night. We slept through it, though.

We aren't taking lessons anymore. I want to go out visiting with Margaret so I can hear more talking. I've been worrying a lot about this language business.

Monday Whitey went out with one of the believers in his broken-down truck. They went to meet Indians but most of the time was spent changing flats. He went out again yesterday and it decided to be stubborn about starting. The man (who owns the truck) knows little about driving or motors and he doesn't have much horse sense about him. I don't like to go out in his truck at all. Ruthie and John Paul love it. Jeanette says he ought to have a car instead of a truck. She remembers a lot about the States. As soon as I get into a routine with the new baby, I hope to give Jeanette the Calvert Kindergarten course. The baby's going to be expensive but we have to do something for her. I hope we can get a desk so she'll have a nice place to study and keep her things.

Our lights came on a week ago Thursday. What a relief concerning the laundry. Our first tank of propane gas lasted 24 days which isn't bad for all the baking I do.

One and a half months more and you'll have 4 grandchildren. Tell Nancy to keep up the good work. I'm tired!

I hope this finds everything a lot better.

Love from us all, Betty

March 23, 1962

Dear Daddy,

I don't know where to begin. Nothing of really earth-shaking importance has happened. Last week the men missionaries went to Manaure but Whitey has written a prayer letter about it.

Last Sunday was elections. All drinking and gatherings were forbidden. The man across the street was elected to a nonpaying position which is desirable as a political stepping stone. He is Liberal - the side that is open to Communism. The Conservatives are strong Catholics and are naturally enemies of communism.

I understand the snow has been melting and causing floods up there.

March 25 - I was interrupted by a visit from David.

April 13th we are going to Barranquilla to wait for the baby. I have no address to give for when we're there so you don't have to write. All I ask is that you get one here before we leave. We will write you however. We found out that we will be able to stay in the Baptist home. It has almost everything furnished. I think we might have to take sheets and towels. We hope to buy about everything for the baby there. We still don't have any names for the baby. I've kind of got it in my head that it's a boy, but I'm likely to be surprised. It would be nice if John Paul could have a brother though.

John Paul gets a lot of attention these days. He says "adios" a lot now. When people pass on the street, the usual greeting is "adios". He also says a recognizable form of "burro" (which is pronounced differently in Spanish) and it sounds cute.

Corwins plan to move into the chapel property in April if it is completed. They wanted to know if we wanted their house. We decided against it for the time being as it would take us too far away from people when we are still struggling with the language.   There are other reasons too, but that's one of the main ones. I can notice improvement in Whitey's talking, but I'm afraid I'm regressing rather than progressing.

Our neighbor across the street was cleaning her drain from the patio and, boy, does it stink. It smells like they must send their bathroom dirt out that drain. Lots of places don't have outhouses even and they just use receptacles that are emptied to the street. Whitey and Mr. Corwin went to Maicao this morning to have a service with the believers there. Sounds like missionary duty, huh?

Whitey is planning how to save so that we might be able to get a jeep next year and get around to different places and meet people. It would be second-hand and John Breman would have to fix it for us. New jeeps cost 20-25 thousand pesos. And that is way out in the dream class.

Jim is 23 today. Your family is getting old. I remember when 20 looked so grownup.

Well, guess that's about it. I hope you're all right and that the weather is kinder.

Love from us all, Betty

P.S. Got John Paul's birthday card all right. Thanks

Letter to a friend...
October 12, 1962

Dear Mrs. Lawrence,

I guess it is about time I answered you. Better late than never (I hope). It was nice to hear your voice on the tape. I'm glad you weren't bashful.

All of the children are getting so big. I am going to start Jeanette soon on the kindergarten course from Culvert Schools. Ruthie is an individualist. She is going to be the white blonde. The others show tendencies of having darker hair. John Paul is quite a guy and will often walk around the house or down the street singing at the top of his lungs. People get a kick out of that. Lynne is almost five months and is chubby.

The rats are playing tag on the roof. While we had our cats we didn't see hide nor hair of a rat. We want to get another. They are scarce and cost money, but they're worth it. Rats can cost plenty by chewing up food and other items.

Whitey is out now trying to get a house to rent in Uribia. We want to move there and start to lean the Indian language. We have to get away entirely from

159

Colombians as the two do not mix. For one thing, the Colombians are more responsive and it is too great a temptation to neglect the Indians. For another the Colombians do not think well of Indians and they just don't mix socially as a rule. The Indians are not educated, but they have no gospel witness and we feel the Lord has called us to them. We need prayer in every respect – moving, learning the language, contacting the Indians, wisdom in dealing with them and gaining their confidence.

I must go now, but may God bless you and keep you well.

Your friend in Christ,
Betty

November 20, 1962

Dear Daddy and Edith,

I'm happy to hear that half the trip was safe and pleasant and I'm assuming the other half was. Nancy had her baby the day you started out, didn't she? I hope it all wasn't too much for her and that you were able to enjoy the visit.

How is Edith doing now? It would be very wonderful if she would try the housekeeping. Please let me know how things are. Too bad she can't come down and help me. I'm glad the tape was all right. I'm still planning to make one myself sometime. Whitey brought the tape recorder back from Riohacha since we have lights all day. We are going to have Mr. Norwood buy a cheap transistor model so that we can take it out to the Wayuu Indians. We will keep this other for tapes for home. Mr. Norwood is coming down in January for conference. To make things easier, we'll all go to Puerto Colombia where we stayed while waiting for Lynne. There won't be any intrusions there.

I'm awfully sorry about your birthday. Moving just took my mind off such things completely. I hope it was a good one though.

The last two weeks there has been an epidemic among the Indians, killing a number and also their animals. They told us it is a kidney disease and is now easing off. However, Whitey seems to be having some kidney trouble and it's rather a worry. We only pray it doesn't get worse. Whitey has been having physical troubles and it is a hindrance as he can't do anything when he's low. Please pray. Nothing is wrong with me that I know of. The kids are pretty good. They don't eat as well as they should, though.

Whitey brought our mother hen back. Someone had turned the nest over and taken her. She broke loose though and rescued one chick. Corvius caught her and kept her for us. She's a good mother. I like to watch them. Reminds me of Psalm 91.

Pray that we will be able to soon get started with the language and that we can find a good informant.

Keep well and keep looking up.

Lots of love from all,
Betty

?, 1962

Dear Daddy and Edith,

I have a problem. We don't have Nancy's address. Would you please send the enclosed letter on to her? You may read it. I do hope you have that address.

It's still terrifically hot and I don't mean maybe. Powells came up for a day's visit and couldn't stand it. They bought a nice '61 Land Rover in Barranquilla and want to visit each station now. We weren't expecting them but it worked out fine except our bathroom is still a mess. Whitey had killed a big rooster that day so I just took the meat off the bones and it served. They had brought meat and some other things with them too.

Sometimes it seems as though we might not make it to the woods. Nothing had actually come in toward that end. Perhaps the Lord doesn't want us there but perhaps we just have to learn patience.

Nancy's package of school books arrived and boy, I'm really getting nervous. Education is so important these days and I'd hate for these kids to have to be put back a year when they go to public schools at home.

We had a broadcast from Havana, Cuba the other night. It was full of hate. The Communists really take advantage of such things. I'm wondering how tomorrow's march on Washington will turn out.

Lynne really suffers from the heat. Between that and her cough she's quite unhappy. At times the phlegm causes her to throw up. We would like to get her checked in Barranquilla but we just don't have money for extra trips. It takes a lot just to eat.

I'm going to let you get other news off of Nancy and Ron's letter. I can hardly keep my eyes open.

Keep well.

Much love, Betty

?. 1963

Dear Daddy and Edith,

The plant's out again and I'm writing by flashlight. I can't seem to find enough time to concentrate in daylight. We do have gas for the stove though. But our bathroom is stopped up (it dribbles out and it's rather a mess). We only flush the toilet in desperation.

Jeanette has reached a milestone. Her teeth are coming out. She'll probably seem to grow even faster now. Boy, I'm really beginning to feel old. It really doesn't seem that long since I lost my teeth and went to kindergarten.

We had Indian dresses made for Jeanette and Ruthie. They look cute and are they proud. They get a lot of attention because Indians with white blond hair are rare.

We finally got gas for the stove. When Whitey goes through Maicao on his way to Fonseca he hopes to get another tank so we won't be caught again. He's going to work on the jeep and I hope this trip finishes it and that we can sell it.

It's been quite warm and we sweat without trying. Lynne, Jeanette, and John Paul have all had colds.

An American girl we met in Riohacha just moved here. Her Colombian husband works for the government and was transferred from Bogota. I haven't seen her yet. I'll let her make the first move because I don't know if she wants to be social. She was Protestant before she was married and is very defensive about being Catholic. They usually are when they change over.

I haven't heard from Jim or Aunt Frances in ages. Nancy is doing better. We just got a package from her that took six months. Customs opened it in Bogota and passed it.

On Tuesday a rat gave birth to six on the kitchen wall. I think she pushed them off on purpose and we swept them out to the chickens. Jeanette was about to keep one. She loves little things. Our hens are doing good and laying some big ones. A little corn makes a lot of difference. Corn is cheaper than eggs.

Today is mail day. Must go but I hope all is well.

Lots of love, Betty

162

March 12, 1963

Dear Daddy and Edith,

Are you melted out by now? I hope you've been making it through safely.

Whitey was gone the whole week. He and John Breman worked on the car several days and it seems it won't take an awful lot to fix. But now Whitey has decided to sell it and buy a refrigerator. John said Land Rovers take a lot of up keep and Whitey doesn't want that. John Paul did pretty well with his daddy, I guess, but he wouldn't let him out of his sight.

Three boys ran off with our cat yesterday. It would seem they are even harder to keep than they are to get. Those very boys made us mad.

There's been a real big change here. We have a 17 year old girl living with us — Adriana Molina from Fonseca. Recommended by Janet Breman. She has cooked, cleaned, and done dishes to date. She has only been here a few days so we aren't really settled yet. It really saves me. Maybe I can gain some weight now especially since I can eat someone else's cooking. She knows the Colombian way, of course, and can fix rice and platano a number of different ways — which I can't. We pay her 100 pesos a month.

I had some hernia trouble. I think it must have been strangulated because I felt it twist and then I began to feel better. We may get it taken care of in Barranquilla next year.

Well, I really can't think of anything else, my mind is just wandering around. It's bedtime. So bye for now. Keep looking up.

Love,
Betty

Summer (?) 1963

Dear Daddy and Edith,

We didn't get any mail last week but we got a double batch this week and it was most gratifying and heartwarming. People have been very responsive to our needs. We hope to be worthy of all the gifts and prayers and concern on our behalf.

Thanks very much for the check. Our support has never been up to par and it's hard to take care of four children on our funds sometimes. We eat, but sometimes shoes and clothing go wanting. I counted our fund left for the quarter and told Whitey we'd probably have to fall back on Christmas money for living expenses.

We have been told of many promises of money to be sent for Christmas. But, best of all, our church sent a letter of inquiry to the mission to find out how much we'll need to move out into the woods. The mission answered them in detail. That is a real answer to prayer.

Glad you had a good time at the "Roundup".

Friday I took the kids over to Effy's and we had a nice visit. The next day she surprised us by coming over and saying "Let's go to Manaure". Well, I was caught off guard so I had to shift into high gear and finally got the kids ready. Whitey wasn't home yet. The road was quite bad in spots and we passed through some mud holes at a 45 degree angle. Just before we got there Jeanette threw up over half the front seat and on one of the little girls. We spent most of the time getting cleaned up. We made it home with Jeanette throwing up in a towel. There were no lights so we had bread and milk for supper by lamplight. Oh well, it was something different for a change!

Whitey finally got home on Monday. He had waited in Maicao for three days and finally decided to go back to Riohacha when a bus driver unexpectedly decided to come up here in a roundabout way. Was I glad to see him! I didn't have any idea when he'd come and it was a surprise. He got the jeep more or less finished. The steering is bad – it has no brakes, etc., but it looks nice, he says. It's up for sale in Riohacha. A believer is acting as an agent and he'll get a commission if he finds a buyer. By the way, around these parts cars (or trucks) without brakes is common. I know any kind of experience is good, like teaching, and I welcome it. But I really have to start from scratch.

Our washing machine won't go. I'm afraid 2 and ½ years of low voltage has taken its toll. A big glob of grease leaked out a couple weeks ago and that's when the trouble really started. Whitey doesn't have tools to take it apart. I don't know what we'll do. It's very discouraging to me. Lack of good mechanics and inaccessible parts are really a problem.

Now that my arm is better I had to take another fall and twisted my foot. I stepped down off the back sidewalk onto a stone I didn't see. It's all rather ridiculous. Now I'm hobbling around with a swollen foot.

Adriana is going home to stay just before Christmas. I wouldn't mind her so much if she could go home every night.

We had real good tuna fish sandwiches and fruit salad for supper. It isn't very often things taste so well.

I hope you're both doing well and keep that way. Bye

Love from all,
Betty

164

November 13, 1963

Dear Daddy and Jim

Your birthday got past me and I'm awfully sorry I forgot. I hope it was pleasant. I'm always apologizing to someone for forgetting their birthday.

I suppose the weather is cool now. We've had it warm and dry but the roads are still recuperating from the rain. We may have more yet.

Monday a group of missionaries and believers met in Maicao for a Bible sell. I guess they all got some strange reactions. Whitey had a bad headache so he had to rest in the hammock part of the time. He got the people in the house all worried.

He saved $10 ($100 pesos) by buying wholesale. Flour, oatmeal, sugar, fat and oil. He also bought a tool so he's going to try and replace grease in the washer. It's been doing better because the voltage has been up. For awhile it was very low.

The man who is trying to sell our jeep is pulling trucks. He is asking a high price and saying the car is two years younger. Next week Whitey is going to see about it and may bring it back if Powells jeep is fixed. Their generator burned out and a replacement isn't immediately available. They have a Land Rover, too, and parts are hard to get. Whitey says some cars and trucks burn out about 5 generators a year. I don't know why it's such a problem here.

The cat that walked away, walked back. At least it seems to be the same. It will probably leave again sometime but I'm not going to worry about it.

Have you got any bandaids laying around so that whenever you send a letter in a regular envelope you could stick one in? Sometimes they would be very helpful.

So long now. I hope you're fine.

Love from all,
Betty

Betty with her father and our five children. This photo was taken on our first furlough in 1965.

Betty and I on our first furlough in 1965.

GLOSSARY

A
Agua...water

Aduana...Customs agency

Alcalde...Mayor of the city

Arrepa...A corn meal, oven baked, muffin-like breakfast food.

Arijunasain...The name given to the windmill nearest our house in Merachon.

Arroyo...A dry river bed that runs with water when it rains.

Atanquez...a town up in the Sierra Nevada Mountains above Valledupar.

B
Barrio...Any part of a city or town. Some cities and towns are made up of many barrios, each with their own name.

Barranquilla...A large city on the Caribbean coastline in northern Colombia. It serves as port of entry when entering the country.

Barro...Mud

Biblia...Bible

Bogota...The capital of Colombia situated high up in the Andes Mountains at about the 10,000 foot level.

C
Cabo de la Vela...Cape of the sail. A high point on the west coast of the Guajira Peninsula. It was reportedly named by Christopher Columbus. From a distance out on the ocean, it looks like a sail.

Camino...road

Carnet...An official document issued by the government but rarely required.

Carraipia...A small hamlet in the Guajira Peninsula situated along the western edge of the foothills of the Andes Mountains near the Venezuelan border

Cedula...An important document issued by the Colombian government for the purpose of identification. It must be carried at all times when outside the house.

Centavos...Money, cents; what we call `change' in English.

Consulate...The premises occupied by a foreign country whose officers and agents are there to promote trade, to protect the rights of their fellow citizens, to issue visas, and to carry out other official duties.

Correo...Mail

Correo postal...The post office

Cucuta...A city on the eastern Colombian/Venezuelan border. When escorting their children to the school in Rubio, Venezuela, the missionaries in Colombia had to pass through this city.

Cuestacita...A check point along the road that connects the towns of Riohacha and Fonseca. There were a few houses, a store and restaurant located there. It is operated by the aduana checking for the passage of contraband from the Guajira Peninsula to points south in the country.

D

DAS...The Colombian department of security. Everybody, both national and foreign, must register with this entity. They issue cedulas which must be carried by everyone who walks the streets.

Departamento...A portion of the country that is equal to a state in the United States. The South America Mission has worked in the states or Departamentos of the Guajira and San Juan de Caesar.

Dinero...Money

E

Embassy...The official headquarters of the ambassador of a foreign country. The U.S. ambassador represents the President of the United States.

Enramada...a Wayuu structure consisting of a roof, open on all sides, and serves as the outdoor living quarters for the Indians. Their houses are for sleeping at night, and are a place to store their possessions. They live mostly outdoors. Visitors are received at an enramada rather than in their houses.

F

FARC...A military resistance force in the country that is disenchanted with the national government.

Fonseca...A farming community located between the Andes and the Sierra Nevada Mountains. The South America Mission established a work in Fonseca as far back as the 1940's. At one time the Mission conducted a Bible Institute to train national pastors. The work has been in the hands of Colombian personnel for many years.

Furlough...A period of time during which missionaries return to the States or Canada for rest, for health reasons, for further education, and to represent the South America Mission in churches and conferences across the country.

G

Guajira...The name of the peninsula on the northernmost part of Colombia. The northern end is mostly desert; the middle part is semi-desert, and the lower part reaches into the foothills of the Andes and Sierra Nevada Mountains ranges.

Getty...Since the Wayuu have no `b' sound in their language, they substitute `g' for `b', so Betty was called Getty. Some substituted the `b' with a `w' so she was also called Wetty. The Wayuu who spoke Spanish used the "b" and called her Betty.

Guava...A tropical fruit.

Guanabana...A tropical fruit.

H

Hammock...The same as in English. It is the most common means for sleeping for both Indians and Colombians. They are made on looms by the Indians, or manufactured commercially and sold in stores. They are quite comfortable if one knows how to sleep in them, namely diagonally.

Himnario...Hymnbook

I

Iglesia...Church

J

Jaguey...A large pit made by bulldozers to catch rain water. These are made by the Colombian government for the benefit of the Wayuu who use the water for drinking, bathing, cooking and watering their animals.

Joven...A young person; a teenager.

Junta...A governing board of any entity.

Junta Directive...A board of directors.

K

Kasachiki...A greeting in the Wayuu language.

M

Manaure...A town on the west coast of the Guajira Peninsula where the Colombian government operates a huge salt business. A Wayuu church has been in existence there since the 1960's and has its own Wayuu Pastor.

Mestizo...A person of mixed blood groups, which in the Guajira peninsula consists mainly of Wayuu and Colombian people.

Molino...An air powered windmill over a drilled well. Over five hundred wells have been drilled and windmills erected for the convenience of the Wayuu, but there are also many windmills that serve the Colombian communities. The wells and windmills are drilled and maintained by the Provision de Agua.

Mucura...A clay water jar, made and used extensively by the Wayuu.

P

Pas y Salvo...An official document issued by the Colombian government indicating that taxes have been paid up to date. This document is needed when leaving the country to show taxes have been paid. It is also needed for major purchases such as the purchase of real estate or motor vehicles.

Peso...Currency, equal to U.S. dollar bills, but of different value.

Primo...A cousin.

Pastor...A preacher.

Pecador...A sinner

Pescador...A fisherman.

Provision de Agua...A government funded company that drills wells, builds water tanks with water troughs, and erects air powered windmills and maintains them, and opens up jagueys. Over five hundred wells and windmills were in operation by 1978. They especially served the Wayuu tribe but also served many of the Colombian towns and villages of the Guajira peninsula.

R

Rancheria...A cluster of houses occupied by an extended family among the Wayuu tribe.

Riohacha...The capital city of the Guajira Peninsula.

S

Sal... Salt, a major export of the Guajira. Canals have been built and large pits have been dug. The canals connect the pits to the ocean. Turbines pump thousands of gallons of water into the pits daily. The water evaporates leaving the salt. The salt is mined by the Wayuu providing income for their labor.

Sarachuii...A site in the Sierra Nevada mountain range, established by Robert and Ruth Ann Moyer in the 1960's to reach the Kogi and Arawac Indian tribes.

Señor...Lord, also equal to the English word for Mister.

Señora… A married woman.

Señorita...An unmarried woman.

Seño...Used in addressing a woman when the marital status is unknoun.

Saludos...Greetings, salutations.

T

Trocha...A trail or path through the woods or across the desert.

U

Uribia.. .A town centrally located on the Guajira Peninsula. It was once the capital of the Guajira, but was too inconvenient to be useful. The Myers lived there during their first term of service. It is now central to the work among the Wayuu tribe. The Provision de Agua is located in Uribia.

V

Valledupar...A large town located on the east side of the Sierra Nevada mountain range in the state of San Juan de Caesar. The South America Mission established a work there in the 1970's.

W

Wayuu...The name by which the Indians call themselves which they say means `the people'. Numbering about 300,000, they are one of South America's larger indigenous tribes. They are often referred as Guajiros.

Y

Yosu...A cactus that grows quite tall and is very useful. Besides the delicious fruit it yields, the center of the cactus is used for thatch on the roofs of Indian houses. It lasts for years and is never thrown away but is reused if a house is dismantled or abandoned.

www.ingramcontent.com/pod-product-compliance
Lightning Source LLC
Chambersburg PA
CBHW081150090426
42736CB00017B/3255